The Art of Writing a PhD Proposal

The Art of Writing a PhD Proposal

A flying start for students and supervisors in the transition from MA to PhD

Hans Sonneveld

Open University Press

Open University Press
McGraw Hill
Unit 4,
Foundation Park
Roxborough Way
Maidenhead
SL6 3UD

email: emea_uk_ireland@mheducation.com
world wide web: www.openup.co.uk

First edition published 2022

Copyright © Open International Publishing Limited, 2022

All rights reserved. Except for the quotation of short passages for the purposes of criticism and review, no part of this publication may be reproduced, stored in a retrieval system, or transmitted, in any form or by any means, electronic, mechanical, photocopying, recording or otherwise, without the prior written permission of the publisher or a licence from the Copyright Licensing Agency Limited. Details of such licences (for reprographic reproduction) may be obtained from the Copyright Licensing Agency Ltd of Saffron House, 6–10 Kirby Street, London EC1N 8TS.

A catalogue record of this book is available from the British Library

ISBN-13: 9780335251568
ISBN-10: 0335251560
eISBN: 9780335251575

Library of Congress Cataloging-in-Publication Data
CIP data applied for

Typeset by Transforma Pvt. Ltd., Chennai, India

Fictitious names of companies, products, people, characters and/or data that may be used herein (in case studies or in examples) are not intended to represent any real individual, company, product or event.

Praise page

"Doctoral proposals are an often-hidden part of the research process, but, as this comprehensive book proves, a strong proposal can make a meaningful contribution to timely completion. Clearly written and based on solid research, this compassionate and practical book is a must for research developers and supervisors. The appendixes will also be useful to anyone about to write their own proposal, especially if their university does not offer sufficient support."
Dr Katherine Firth, The University of Melbourne, Australia, author of How to Fix your Academic Writing Trouble: A Practical Guide and Your PhD Survival Guide: Planning, Writing and Succeeding in your Final Year

"This informative and interesting book ends where most others, giving academic advice to potential PhD students, begin. Sonneveld describes in detail the concept of a Proposal Laboratory. This is an extended Workshop for producing an acceptable, high level Research Proposal. Help in writing the Proposal, which will determine whether an applicant is accepted to continue to registration for a research degree, is a much needed addition to this field. Based on years of experience and research he illustrates with clear diagrams and tables the developing process through which the participants must pass. Supervisors and decision makers will find it exciting to discover new areas for guiding hopeful research candidates on their journey."
Dr Estelle M Phillips, Co-author How to Get a PhD, Former Research Tutor Birkbeck College, University of London, UK and Independent Educational Consultant

"Embarking on a PhD trajectory is one of those things you normally do once in a lifetime, so for most it is uncharted territory. Therefore this book by Hans Sonneveld is very timely and useful to all who aspire to gain the title of Doctor (of Philosophy), but also for (potential) supervisors who want to guide their PhD candidates, individually or in a network, towards a top-notch but doable PhD project."
Dr Paul M. van Dijk, Director, Twente Graduate School, University of Twente, Netherlands

"Universities are concerned about delays and low completion rates in doctoral studies. But too often, insufficient attention is paid to the initial phase, when candidates struggle to develop a solid research proposal. Hans Sonneveld's book The Art of Writing a PhD Proposal fills a neglected gap in the literature. Step by step, he reveals how we can *implement the idea of the Proposal Lab to professionally support our doctoral candidates in this challenging endeavour. Together with the rich material in the appendices and the tips for further reading, this makes his book a valuable resource for doctoral school leaders, supervisors, professionals and doctoral candidates alike. He states that "learning how to plan a proposal and then conduct dissertation research will change the life of doctoral candidates." If we apply his approach, we can contribute to this change."*

Lucas Zinner, Head of Research Services and Career Development, University of Vienna, Austria, Chair of the Board of the Association of Professionals in Doctoral Education (PRIDE)

"A welcome resource which will resonate with new and experienced PhD supervisors alike. This book, based on a well-established taught course, has the strength of tried and tested teaching methods and subject content. I especially appreciate the concept of a process, which clearly focusses on the journey as well as the end product. I also, particularly like the practical nature of the book, along with the clear theoretical underpinnings, which, I feel, enables supervisors to clearly guide their students through the proposal stage. Overall, this is a welcome addition to the research literature, available."

Dr Mary Knight, Honorary Senior Lecturer (Education), University of Dundee, UK

"Writing a good proposal is key to PhD success. The Art of Writing a PhD Proposal provides an indispensable guide to this important, and often neglected, part of the PhD process. For students, it gives a practical, step-by-step plan for creating a proposal that will be both convincing to supervisors, and helpful in planning the PhD journey. For universities, it explains how to run 'Proposal Lab' sessions to engage students actively in devising and planning high-quality research. A wealth of material, such as questionnaires and workshop handouts, is included, which will be useful to PhD course directors around the world."

Dr Colin Johnson, University of Nottingham, UK, co-author of the 7th edition of How to Get a PhD

Contents

Preface		x
	Personal background	x
	Early attrition and serious delay	x
	Proposal secrets	xii
	The Proposal Lab and this handbook	xiii
	Roadmap for the reader	xiii
Acknowledgements		xv

1	SUPPORTING OUR STUDENTS AND EARLY PHD CANDIDATES ON THE WAY TO A PHD PROPOSAL	1
	1 Introduction	1
	2 Organizing the support of (potential) PhD candidates	2
2	THE PROPOSAL LAB PRINCIPLES	12
	1 Introduction	12
	2 Some didactic considerations	17
	3 Proposal Lab objectives	22
	4 Admission to the programme	23
	5 The prospectus, the journey, and the calendar	25
	6 The literature	30
3	THE JOURNEY TO THE PHD PROPOSAL: THE STUDENTS' PERSPECTIVE	31
	1 Introduction: roadmap for the readers	31
	2 Different paths lead to a PhD proposal	33
	3 The map: an overview of the journey to the proposal	36
	4 The basics of our journey	36
	5 Our guides: the supervisors and the Proposal Lab conveners	46
	6 The preconditions	53
	7 The stages	54
	8 Anticipating problems and concerns	70
	9 What we will know at the end of the proposal journey	78
4	THE PROPOSAL LAB SESSIONS AND FEEDBACK MEETINGS	80
	1 Session 1: in search of our research topic	80
	2 The first individual feedback meeting: getting a feeling for your student's qualities and interests	86
	3 Session 2: meeting and interviewing researchers and planning the proposal	93
	4 Session 3: the PhD proposal	100
	5 Session 4: searching for the important literature	106
	6 Session 5: the literature review	114

	7 The second individual feedback meeting: the well-reasoned topic choice	119
	8 Session 6: from topic to questions	121
	9 Session 7: theory, hypothesis and claim	124
	10 Session 8: the research design	128
	11 The third individual feedback meeting: the Proposal Halfway	134

5 WHAT WE WILL KNOW AFTER COMPLETION OF THE PROPOSAL LAB — 135

1 Different types of proposal writers — 135
2 Predicting underperforming in proposal writing: is it possible? — 136

APPENDICES — 143

APPENDIX A. THE WRITING OF A PROPOSAL AND BEING A PHD CANDIDATE: LITERATURE TIPS FOR TEACHERS, SUPERVISORS, STUDENTS AND PHD CANDIDATES — 145

APPENDIX B. EXAMPLE OF A PROPOSAL LAB PROSPECTUS — 148

1 Overview of Proposal Lab objectives — 148
2 Lab objectives in detail — 149
3 Lab requirements — 149
4 Extract of a literature review, based on at least five texts — 152
5 Research question and embedding report — 152
6 Interview report — 153
7 Literature search report — 153
8 Evaluation criteria for Proposal Halfway and Final Proposal — 153

APPENDIX C. EXAMPLE OF A PROPOSAL LAB SCHEDULE (SEPTEMBER–JUNE) — 154

APPENDIX D. THE SNAPSHOT: STUDENTS' INFORMATION ABOUT RESEARCH INTERESTS — 160

Research interest and topic(s) under consideration (max. 1000 words in total) — 160

APPENDIX E. THE ROUGH TOPIC EXPLORATION: IN-CLASS ASSIGNMENT, SESSION 1 — 163

The Rough Topic Exploration Matrix, in-class assignment — 163

APPENDIX F. PLANNING THE WELL-REASONED TOPIC CHOICE AND PROPOSAL DESIGN: IN-CLASS ASSIGNMENT, SESSION 2 — 165

APPENDIX G. PROPOSAL INFORMATION AND TIPS: SESSION 3 — 169

1 Writing the proposal abstract — 169
2 Rubrics for evaluating the proposal qualities — 170
3 Criteria for evaluating research questions — 175

APPENDIX H. A WELL-REASONED TOPIC CHOICE: GUIDELINES FOR STUDENTS AND PHD CANDIDATES	177
APPENDIX I. INSTRUCTIONS IN FORM FORMAT FOR WRITING THE PROPOSAL HALFWAY	179
1 Give a brief description of your project	179
2 The research question	180
3 The innovative character of the proposed project	181
4 Considerations regarding theory and prior research	182
5 Proposition, hypotheses and concepts	182
6 The data and methods	183
7 Additional information	183
APPENDIX J. THE DISCIPLINARY EMBEDDING ASSIGNMENT, SESSION 4 AND SESSION 5	184
Disciplinary embedding: area/theme/subject/essential others	184
APPENDIX K. THE QUESTION PRACTICUM: SESSION 6	186
Checklist for the elaboration into sub-questions	188
APPENDIX L. EVALUATING INDIVIDUAL RESEARCH TRAINING ASSIGNMENTS	189
1 Evaluation of interview reports	189
2 Evaluation of the literature search report	190
3 Evaluation of the critical appraisals	191
4 The evaluation of a literature review	193
APPENDIX M. SWOT ANALYSIS BY CANDIDATES ALREADY HALFWAY TO A PROPOSAL (THE CLINIC)	195
APPENDIX N. EXPECTATIONS IN VIEW OF A 4 YEAR PHD PROJECT	196
APPENDIX O. PLANNING MATRIX PHD TRAJECTORY: RESEARCH AND OTHER ACTIVITIES	201
APPENDIX P. AT THE END OF THE PROPOSAL JOURNEY: SWOT ANALYSIS IN VIEW OF A (FUTURE) PHD PROJECT	204
APPENDIX Q. TRAINING AND SUPERVISION PLAN	206
Bibliography	211
Index	214

Preface

Personal background

The world of doctoral programmes has fascinated me for years. I was director of a Dutch graduate school and during those 18 years I also obtained my doctoral degree based on a study entitled 'Supervisors, PhD candidates and the academic selection' (Sonneveld, 1997). I studied, among other things, the big problems of dropout and delay. Years later, I picked up those themes again in research into PhD candidates who faced extreme delay and candidates whose dissertation was initially rejected. An overarching theme in all my work has always been the insufficient support in the transition to the next phase of study and the tacit assumption that our candidates already had the required qualities and skills.

My focus slowly shifted to preventing these problems. I evaluated the supervision and working conditions of PhD candidates at several universities. The next, logical step was to provide support programmes for supervisors and PhD candidates. The result of this was the publication of several guides for PhD supervisors and the organization of workshops on specific themes for PhD candidates. Prevention *in ultima forma* took the form of a programme that I provided for five years for Master's students who were preparing a PhD project: the Proposal Lab. The handbook before you makes this approach accessible to students preparing for PhD research, their PhD supervisors and programme directors seeking answers to the issues of: (1) early attrition; (2) serious delay; (3) the embedding of doctoral candidates who move from another location to new surroundings; and (4) well-thought-out decisions about whether to start a doctoral trajectory.

Early attrition and serious delay

Attrition, serious delay, and insufficient preparation for a doctoral project are global phenomena. British research reports on the major problem of the early departure of PhD candidates who have just started their PhD research. This affects 16.2 per cent (4.224) of the PhD candidates who started their PhD research between 2006 and 2017! The study states:

> There are many reasons why a student may decide to leave a programme early .... The individual may no longer believe undertaking a PhD is for them ... [or] may face unforeseen problems beyond their control, such as poor health, bereavement, or family difficulties, preventing them from completing their research.
>
> (DiscoverPhDs, 2021)

Remarkably, these authors do not mention the reasons that take the form of poor preparation for a PhD programme, an unprofessional admission procedure, and insufficient supervision and support during the development of a PhD proposal.

This disregard is consistent with the problem raised by Bowen and Rudenstine and Lovitts in the USA who studied the enormous premature outflow from American PhD programmes:

> Data on attrition prior to the start of the second year show a ... pattern over time, with roughly 25 percent of entering students at larger programmes failing to return for the second year and ... 10 to 15 percent of students in smaller programmes leaving at this stage.
> (Bowen and Rudenstine, 1992: 252)

They point to a structural shortcoming in the preparation of aspiring PhD candidates or early-stage PhD candidates for the transition to conducting independent research:

> There is too little emphasis during the first two years on helping students to understand what it means to do independent research ... They are taught to be analytic and critical without necessarily acquiring the habits of mind and training to undertake more constructive and fruitful research and writing.
> (ibid.: 254)

Almost ten years later, Lovitts puts it this way:

> The first task in the research stage [of a PhD] involves finding a research question or thesis topic ... No Director of Graduate Study or faculty member mentioned helping students understand how to conduct thesis research. Their silence on this issue suggests they assume that students know how to proceed.
> (2001: 73)

A special case is the Dutch situation. Some 56 per cent of scientific research is financed by the Dutch Research Council (24 per cent) or third parties (32 per cent). This means that most PhD candidates in the Netherlands start their PhD research based on a plan not written by them and usually developed at least one year previously. They must update the project design and assess it qualitatively. This means that they must appropriate the proposed project.

An important characteristic of doing a PhD in the Netherlands is also that 40 per cent of PhD candidates come from abroad. Here the issue of the transition to a different academic culture plays a vital role. They often arrive with their own rudimentary research plan that sufficed as an entrance ticket but will certainly have to be developed further.

The greatest completion rate damage is incurred in the Netherlands due to the delay in completing the theses. Only 10 per cent of PhD candidates in the

Netherlands obtain their PhD within 4 years. On average, dissertation projects take 10 months longer than planned. I undertook research into the problem of the long PhD duration in a specific faculty. What was the result? At the end of the second year, it was already clear that the dissertation would not be ready on time, but no hard measures were taken, neither by the candidate nor the supervisors. Delayed decisions on essential parts of the dissertation, such as the leading research question and the theoretical framework, played a key role. There was also a lack of structuring of the research. It was striking that there was no question of an unhappy relationship with the supervisor. However, in the opinion of the PhD candidates, the supervisors should have taken on the role of coach and process supervisor much more thoroughly. This situation was an important reason for the faculty in question to start preparing the PhD research in the Master's programme via the Proposal Lab (Sonneveld, 2015).

Proposal secrets

There is not a single book about the art of teaching and guiding young researchers who want to write a PhD proposal. Yes, we do have books about the characteristics of a research proposal and books with tips and tricks for PhD candidates who are facing that challenge. Aspiring PhD candidates are always advised: prepare a PhD proposal, but it is never explained which path will lead to that proposal. Books on supervision and teaching in preparatory studies consider a one-page information sheet on the components of a proposal to be sufficient. For the rest, dear students, and supervisors, find out for yourself!

For example, in *Effective Postgraduate Supervision* by Eley and Jennings (2005) the proposal does not even appear at all. The same goes for *Mastering Your PhD*, by Gosling and Noordam (2006), written for PhD candidates, but not paying any attention to the proposal.

It is quite different in the case of Brewer's (2007) *Your PhD Thesis* and Punch's (2016) *Developing Effective Research Proposals*. An entire chapter and a complete book respectively are devoted to the Research Proposal, however, but still without suggesting a plan for how to get from a vague research interest to a detailed proposal with which one can apply for a PhD position or successfully complete the first stage of the PhD trajectory.

For me, the work of Barbara Lovitts is crucial. In 2007, Barbara Lovitts published her outstanding text, *Making the Implicit Explicit: Creating Performance Expectations for the Thesis*. Her book is about making explicit to students the tacit 'rules' for the assessment of the final of all educational products: the thesis, and its starting point, the proposal. The purpose of defining performance expectations is to make them transparent to graduate students while they are in the research and writing phases, and thus help them achieve higher levels of accomplishment. Analogous to this approach, this handbook therefore hopefully fills a gap that is present in the existing supervision literature by making the proposal requirements and the path to a proposal more explicit.

Preface **xiii**

The Proposal Lab and this handbook

This handbook is based on a programme that I ran with colleagues for five years for Dutch and Belgian Research Master's students at Tilburg University. It was part of a major change in the organization of Dutch university education. In addition to the regular Master's programmes, Research Master's programmes were created in numerous places in which students were specially prepared for a research career. A programme aimed at developing a research proposal is a core component. An important goal is to improve the transition from the existing course programmes to a new phase in which initiative and independence are central to the students. In this preliminary stage of a PhD training, students can discover whether preparing a long-term research project is really something for them. For the supervisors and graduate schools, this means that they have seen students working on a research plan for several months and that it is possible to make a well-considered judgement on whether the student will be admitted to the PhD track and who can best function as the primary supervisor.

The main aim of this handbook is to clarify how to support (potential) PhD candidates in making decisions about a research topic and how to teach them the secrets of a great research proposal, within a well-planned time schedule.

This book follows the structure of a travel guide. It starts with the exploration of possible topics, the move from topics to questions, the positioning of oneself in a specific field of research, exploring supervision possibilities and ends with the proud presentation of a doable PhD research project.

The Proposal Lab is designed to provide faculty guidance and peer support for the development of (1) an elaborated research proposal as a stand-alone exercise, or (2) the basic material for an application for a PhD position or a research position outside academia. Parallel to the Proposal Lab, students will engage in intensive co-operation with members of the faculty, research group or graduate school who are experts on their topic. The Proposal Lab *is not* a substitute for specialized training in particular disciplinary topics, which may be expected from teachers in domain courses and potential future supervisors.

Roadmap for the reader

This book has six main components. In Chapter 1, I indicate that there can be several paths that can lead to a PhD proposal. The most important distinction is that between individual guidance by a supervisor and a workshop or community of practice-like setting, which I refer to in this book as the Proposal Lab. This chapter is primarily aimed at the supervisors, those who are responsible for setting up the PhD trajectory and in particular the programme teams who want to develop taught elements in the programme.

Chapter 2 focuses on the Proposal Lab Principles. I outline the background of the programme, the goals, the didactic foundations, the qualities that students are bringing and the structure of the lab. This chapter is primarily aimed at colleagues supervising a Proposal Lab and programme developers considering introducing such a community of practice. If students are considering a PhD programme that includes a Proposal Lab-like programme, this chapter offers them tools to get a grip on its quality.

In Chapter 3, I describe the journey to a proposal as a travel guide from the students' and candidates' perspective. I inform the travellers about the best preparation, the stages, the must-see attractions, the composition of the travel group and any complications that may arise. Although the emphasis in this handbook is on the Proposal Lab, we broaden the perspective here. In the first place, this chapter is intended for both students and early PhD candidates preparing a proposal within the context of a Proposal Lab or community of practice, as well as candidates who do this on their own with the support of a supervisor. Supervisors can take note of the advice that advanced PhD students give to the beginners, and the advice of supervisors to colleagues who are supervising proposal writers.

In Chapter 4, I outline the sessions of the Proposal Lab, consisting of eight sessions and three individual feedback meetings. For each session, the readers will find a script, the most important substantive suggestions, assignments, and instruments with which the PhD candidates can get started. This chapter is written from the perspective of the Proposal Lab convener. In terms of content, it is also of direct importance for the participants in the Lab, individual students, and PhD candidates who are preparing a PhD proposal, and their supervisors.

Chapter 5 discusses the results of this Proposal Lab. What do students and supervisors learn about the enthusiasm and suitability that are essential for a PhD track that will take at least 4 years? This chapter informs supervisors, Proposal Lab conveners and students about the results of the Proposal Lab and the qualities needed for a successful dissertation process.

Finally, an important component of the book is the Appendices. There readers will find many tools that are of direct use for writing the proposal and supervising it.

An important caveat to conclude. As you will see, I have enjoyed the work of many colleagues from a wide variety of disciplines. In several cases I advised my students to study the important books in that particular discipline. Consider these references as suggestions. Regarding the substantive themes that I cover in the sessions of the Proposal Lab, you may have excellent alternatives that are more focused on your discipline. Take advantage of those, of course. Use my suggestions as a checklist to assess whether the essential points that play a role in writing a proposal are also covered in your preferred alternatives.

Acknowledgements

This book would not have been possible without the important work of my colleagues Heinze Oost, who sadly passed away much too young, and Angela Markenhof. Years ago, they published four small guides on preparing, supervising, and conducting research, and reporting on it afterwards. They laid the foundation for supervising the start of a PhD research project on which I could build.

I would also like to mention Rob van Gestel, with whom I provided the first versions of this Proposal Lab for Research Master's students from the universities of Tilburg and Leuven. We didn't agree on everything, but the collaboration was essential to the ideas developed in this book.

There are also colleagues who have given me enormous encouragement to realize this book. I mention here: Melita Kovačević (Zagreb University), Lucas Zinner (University of Vienna), Joris Veenhoven (University of Utrecht), Paul van Dijk (University of Twente), Inge van der Weijden (Center for Science and Technology Studies, University of Leiden) and two anonymous reviewers. Their contributions have resulted in a major enrichment of the handbook. It now addresses both the supervisors and tutors of PhD candidates as well as those candidates themselves.

And where would this handbook have been without the intense, determined, and open-minded support of the colleagues at the Open University Press? In chronological order Sam Crowe, Beth Summers, Bryony Waters, Hannah Jones, Hannah Cartwright, Susan Dunsmore and Maureen Cox.

I am grateful to them all.

# Supporting our students and early PhD candidates on the way to a PhD proposal

> **Reading tip**
>
> This chapter is primarily aimed at the supervisors, those who are responsible for setting up the PhD trajectory and in particular the programme teams who want to develop taught elements in the programmes leading to a PhD trajectory.

1 Introduction

Different paths can lead to a PhD project. There is a supervisor's research plan, for which money is available and for which a suitable PhD candidate is sought. There are the MA students or early PhD candidates who can submit their own proposal and obtain funding on that basis. There are the foreign PhD candidates who have their own plan and who bring their own funding.

Various starting positions are also conceivable regarding the timing of the PhD project. For example, there are candidates who will combine their PhD project with a job or other activities. They work part-time on their PhD research and will take longer than their full-time colleagues. What these candidates share is that they can either write a good PhD proposal themselves, or they must be able to appropriate and specify a research plan written by their supervisor.

How can the university or graduate school best organize the introduction and admission of all these different types of candidates?

2 Organizing the support of (potential) PhD candidates

2.1 Triage: at what stage is our candidate?

The type of programme we are going to offer depends on the personal situation of the potential participants. The biggest difference is that between the 'absolute beginners' and those who are already well on their way to a research proposal. The latter can take two forms: they have previously written a draft of a proposal or have been selected to implement a plan developed by their supervisor.

In the case of the absolute beginners, participation in our Proposal Lab is the way to go, unless you want to place their proposal development entirely in the hands of individual supervisors.

In the second case, candidates who are well on their way, a Clinic model is obvious. The participants attend a Clinic, present their research plan in the making, receive feedback, and can determine whether the required skills are present. They can work on missing skills via a Mini Course, after which a definitive plan is drawn up and discussed in the Clinic.

2.2 Before starting the PhD research

It is beneficial to have prospective PhD candidates work on a PhD plan in an earlier study phase. The students can investigate whether they really want to start a PhD project and whether they have enough drive to investigate a certain topic. In this phase, the student can also investigate which supervisor best fits the interest and personality of the future PhD candidate. If the students have drafted a good thesis plan at the end of this exploration phase, they will be off to a flying start in the PhD trajectory. This reduces the risk of a doctoral research lasting too long, with all the associated risks for successful completion. This test phase is easy to realize for the Master's or MA students of the faculty where they can move on to a PhD position and the early-stage American PhD candidates.

A complication can arise when internal candidates work on a thesis plan for which no finances are available afterwards. This can occur in countries where universities do not have the resources to finance PhD research themselves. PhD candidates and supervisors are then dependent on finances from the second and third funding stream (national science organizations or non-academic clients). Nevertheless, drafting your own research plan is of great value as a learning experience, even though the subject may have to be changed later. The PhD candidates who have had such a pre-PhD experience will be perfectly prepared to take a project into their own hands for which the supervisor, for example, has laid the foundation.

In some cases, students interested in a PhD trajectory can also be invited to participate in such an orientation programme, without a decision having already been made on the allocation of the PhD position. An example is the English MPhil programme that determines whether the candidate may switch to a PhD programme.

2.3 During the first year of a PhD trajectory

In the case of internal or external candidates who have not followed a preparatory proposal training, it is of value to make the Proposal Lab part of their first year of the PhD trajectory. They can familiarize themselves with several research and study skills that will prove to be of great value later. Consider, for example, the refinement of the research questions, engaging the most important literature, reflection on the methods of data collection, the timing of the trajectory, the planning of interim products in the form of journal articles and conference contributions and the explication of the requirements that will be imposed on a thesis. This helps not only the PhD candidate but also the supervisors, as part of the PhD training is taken off their hands.

2.4 A big difference: a candidate's own plan or a plan by the supervisor

It does matter whether PhD candidates are working on their own PhD plan or have been hired to carry out a supervisor's research plan. Table 1.1 shows the differences in aspects.

Table 1.1 Differences between the sources of PhD plan

Aspect	PhD candidates working on their own research plan	Doctoral candidates hired to implement supervisor's plan
Research topic	Doctoral candidate chooses a subject based on personal interest	Topic is fixed to a greater or lesser extent. With a wide scope of definition, PhD candidates will have to clarify and specify
Connection with the literature	Doctoral candidate will map the most important literature based on recognized search strategies. To be checked by supervisors	The research plan, including literature references, was often written a year or more ago. The doctoral candidates will have to investigate whether new, recent studies have now come to light. In that case too, the PhD candidates must be familiar with recognized search strategies
The literature review	Doctoral candidates will have to familiarize themselves with the requirements that are set for a literature review. In every thesis, or part of it, treatment of the relevant literature is essential	Doctoral candidates will have to familiarize themselves with the requirements that are set for a literature review. In every thesis, or part of it, treatment of the relevant literature is essential

(Continued)

Table 1.1 (Continued)

Aspect	PhD candidates working on their own research plan	Doctoral candidates hired to implement supervisor's plan
Central research questions and sub-questions	Doctoral candidates must familiarize themselves with the requirements of relevance, transparency and coherence that are placed on a good research question and the sub-questions	Based on this knowledge of requirements, the doctoral candidates must assess whether the research questions meet the criteria
The data that the research must provide	Doctoral candidate determines what information is needed to answer the research questions. To be checked by supervisors	The supervisor usually has a good picture of the data to be collected. The doctoral students check whether the mentioned data still match the possibly modified research questions
Methods of data collection	The PhD candidate determines the methods of data collection. To be checked by supervisors	The PhD candidates check whether the methods mentioned in the research plan are adequate
The structure of the thesis and the requirements that it must meet	The PhD candidates present a provisional table of contents and knows what requirements are set for, for example, Introduction, Literature Review and Conclusions. To be checked by supervisors	The PhD candidates present a provisional table of contents and know what requirements are set for, for example, Introduction, Literature Review and Conclusions. To be checked by supervisors
The planning of the investigation	The PhD candidates are primarily responsible for the planning of the research and the interim products. To be checked by supervisors	If all goes well, the supervisor has made the planning workable. The PhD candidates checks whether the timely completion of the thesis according to this plan is plausible

Here we see how proposal training can support the PhD candidates in making their own research plan or enables them to assess a supervisor's plan and to specify it if necessary.

2.5 The individual track: supervisors accompany their own PhD candidate

Imagine that you are supervising a PhD candidate who has not drafted a thesis plan in a previous study phase or who cannot participate in a Proposal Lab in the first year of the PhD programme. Although this handbook is focused on supporting PhD candidates in the context of a Proposal Lab, you will find many building blocks for supporting your PhD candidate in drafting a good research plan.

Here I outline the stages you are likely to go through with your candidate. For each item you will find tools in the Appendices of this handbook that can help you and your candidate.

On the way to a proposal: overview

Table 1.2 Overview of stages in the PhD journey

Topic	Activity	Available tools and information
Getting to know your candidate	Information sources: • Use earlier experiences with the candidate, products of earlier research activities (MA thesis!) and the Snapshot • Interview your candidate regarding this material	Appendix D: The Snapshot
Composition of the supervision team	Consider broadening the supervision team if it consists of only one supervisor up to now. In some countries the supervision may not be by one and only supervisor.	
How far the candidates is on the way to a proposal	Discussion of the journey to a proposal	Figure 3.1
Skills and knowledge in action		
Planning	Planning the journey to the proposal	Flowcharts as presented in Appendix F
Meeting other experts	Interviewing + writing draft of interview invitation + writing of interview report. Discussion with you about the report	Appendix L: Section 1, evaluation of interview reports
Literature search	If necessary, the candidate reads literature on how to do a literature search and literature review	Appendix L: and Session 5 of the Proposal Lab:

(Continued)

Table 1.2 (Continued)

Topic	Activity	Available tools and information
Critical appraisal of scientific work	The candidate will practise a literature search and critical appraisal of literature. The candidate will write a literature review of five texts and a report on the search process	Section 2, Evaluation of the literature search report, Section 3, Evaluation of the critical appraisals, Section 4, Evaluation of the literature reviews
Literature review	Discussion with you about the test review	
Writing skills	You will analyse strengths and weaknesses in earlier study products of your candidate. Option: candidate participates in courses such as Academic Publishing	
Getting a grip on the basic components of a research proposal	Reading: • Reading two examples of research proposals and discussing them with you • Interviewing peers who did write a proposal • Reading one of the many proposal guidelines	Appendices G and I Session 3 of the Proposal Lab
Distinguishing different types of research questions	Discussing with you the results of the Question Practicum	Appendix K: The Question Practicum
The well-reasoned topic choice	Meeting your candidate to discuss the topic preferences	Appendix H: A Well-Reasoned Topic Choice
An essential moment: giving your candidate insight into your expectations regarding the planning of the process towards a proposal and the quality criteria you will use	Basic thought: a thorough proposal can be finished in 6–7 months. Ask your candidate to fill in the flowchart	Appendix F

(Continued)

Table 1.2 (Continued)

Topic	Activity	Available tools and information
Getting a grip on the proposal and thesis quality criteria	a. Reading the applicable chapter of Lovitts (2007) *Making the Implicit Explicit* b. Evaluating two theses c. If the candidate will be doing research for which you composed the original outline: ask your candidate to evaluate the research design and to update the literature review	Appendix G: Rubrics for evaluating the proposal qualities
From topic to question	The translation of research interests into the questions that will guide the research. Discussing the relevant section of the proposal with your candidate	Appendix K : The Question Practicum
The question of originality	Discussing Lamont's 28 ways to be original (Lamont, 2009)	Reading information of Session 8 (Originality and relevance). Discussing the relevant section of the proposal
Theory – claim – working hypothesis	Discussing Booth et al. (2016): Making an Argument and the information of Session 7	Discussing the relevant section of the proposal
Research design	Reading the information of Session 8 (The research design)	Discussing the relevant section of the proposal
Proposal Halfway	Offering feedback to your student/PhD candidate as to the Proposal Halfway	Making use of Appendices G and I
Final Proposal	Discussing and evaluating the result, The Proposal	Making use of Appendices G and I

Many issues in Table 1.2 will look familiar to you. Or you may even assume that your PhD candidate is familiar with them. If your PhD candidate does indeed have all this knowledge, the overview in Table 1.2 can serve as a checklist that you go through with your PhD candidate. You will come across some points that may be new to your PhD candidate. An important feature of this check is that important aspects of the PhD track are made explicit and you do not implicitly assume that they are known by your PhD candidate. Consider, for example, the moment at which an Introduction for the thesis is written. Your doctoral candidate will assume that this is the very last part of the writing process. However, you know how fruitful it is to write a draft-of-a draft-of-an-introduction during the first thesis year. This will then have the function of a compass for the entire process that will be adjusted and adjusted again while working.

A special variant of this individual approach is the collaboration between a supervisor and a Master's student in designing a research plan for which they can apply for an external grant. In this case, too, the following can take a lot of work away from the supervisor. There is a risk that the proposal will not receive funding. In such a case, the PhD candidate can also submit the proposal if, for example, a university PhD position becomes available. Even if all that fails, this experience in writing a proposal is of great value. For example, if the PhD candidate applies for a PhD position for which a project description is already available, this candidate will be perfectly prepared for a meeting with a selection committee to discuss the project and the opportunities for improvement. After all, the candidate is perfectly capable of seeing the strengths and weaknesses of a proposal.

2.6 A special option: a programme for external PhD candidates

A special category of potential PhD candidates is those who no longer follow a university programme but want to investigate from an employment position whether a PhD is something for them. Also in this case, a Proposal Lab is optimal. I developed such a programme for ten employees of Berenschot, an independent, international management consultancy firm. The programme developed into a pilot study in combining a tough consulting job and working on a thesis plan simultaneously. Interesting research ideas were developed, but at the end of the six months of the programme it was clear to all the participants and the Berenschot management that to actually start the thesis trajectory was impossible without a major adjustment of the professional work in terms of time.

2.7 The Clinic annex mini course

In fact, there are three variants in the guidance of a proposal development. In the first place, there is the support for potential PhD candidates in the form of the Proposal Lab. Second, there is the individual trajectory of supervisor and PhD candidate. Third, there is the Clinic model in which the participants – those who are already further down the road – analyse the progress of their proposal and determine with the Clinic's convener what work is still to be done. This is a time-focused programme where knowledge and skills are tested, and the emphasis is much less on their acquisition. In some cases, a limited form of remedial teaching is the appropriate way. The starting point is a proposal in the making.

Table 1.3 Clinic, Session I: the state of affairs

Getting to know each other	Introduction by convener. Information for participants as regards the further plan of action. Participants to inform the convener about their situation: • How far are they down the road to the definite version of a PhD proposal? • What has been done? • What is still to be done?

Data collection	In Clinic activity: candidates perform a SWOT analysis regarding what they know about the supervisor's expectations and the presence or absence of necessary skills (see Appendix M, 'SWOT analysis by candidates already halfway to a proposal'). What do the participants know about their supervisor's expectations?
	• In terms of *the timing* of the project
	• In terms of *the thesis format*
	  o Will the thesis be a book?
	  o Will the thesis be composed of journal articles?
	  o If so, how many articles?
	  o Are there special requirements on the status of the journals?
	  o What is the supervisor's opinion regarding the necessary or unnecessary coherence between the components of the thesis?
	  o What will be the number of articles?
	  o What is the aspired journal status?
	3. In terms of *quality criteria that will apply* to the proposal.
	In case of more than one supervisor: the agreements between the supervisors regarding the issues mentioned above.
	Knowledge. What does the participant know about:
	• the financial conditions of the project?
	• the agreements about co-authorship?
	Analysis of *skills, knowledge* of:
	• Planning – flowcharts
	• How to get from Topic to Question
	• Literature search
	• Critical appraisal
	• Literature review
	• Role of theory/hypothesis/claim
	• Proposal Format
	• Research design in the participant's discipline
	• Quality criteria applicable to proposal
	• Operationalization of the Originality criterion
	• '80% ready model' versus paralyzing perfectionism
	• How to manage supervisors

(Continued)

Table 1.3 (Continued)

Conclusions: determination of strengths and weaknesses in the current situation + developing plan of action:	
Improvement strategies for weaker aspects	• Extra skills training? • Reading skills literature, searching, and reading important website information? • Peer support? • Contact with supervisor?
Timing of activities between first and second Clinic sessions	Making a flowchart. Is there a product that they would like to work on and discuss in Session 2 of this Clinic?
Example of a strategy	In the clinic, a discussion of a research proposal, with application of previously sent literature about proposal criteria

Table 1.4 Clinic Session 2: results of improvement strategies

Evaluation of flowchart	Evaluation per participant
Situation as regards major improvement actions	Reporting per participant
Convener evaluates per participant: the situation, and suggestions	
Further action intentions of the participants for the near future	
Brain gymnastics	• Writing a blurb of the thesis as it could look in 4 years • Machine Trick: what is the best way to end my thesis without success? (See Chapter 3, Section 8.4)

A programme for a Clinic in two sessions can look as shown in Table 1.3 and Table 1.4. The reader will see that many building blocks correspond 1-to-1 with the components of the Proposal Lab that will be discussed in detail in the following chapters.

2.8 A collective approach: the Proposal Lab as a community of practice

There are many good reasons to get Master's students or first-year PhD candidates working in groups on a thesis plan. They will support each other in many areas and will also hold a mirror up to each other. 'Best practices' of participants are a source of inspiration for them all. Another advantage of a Proposal Lab is that the supervisors have a lot of work taken off their hands. Searching for the important literature, writing the literature review, learning how to present your research, planning a research project and getting a grip on the requirements for a thesis can be efficiently transferred to the Proposal Lab context. This does not mean that the individual (prospective) supervisors do not play an important role. When it comes to the specific content of the research and the data collection, they are the first discussion partners for the (prospective) PhD candidates. It is interesting that the participants in the Proposal Lab can be supported in the choice of supervisors, but also in taking responsibility in the supervision process.

My approach has many similarities with the community of practice approach that revolves around individuals who share the same concern or passion for an activity and take the initiative to improve themselves in doing the activity as they communicate on a regular basis. Three dimensions characterize the community of practice, namely: (1) mutual engagement; (2) joint enterprise; and (3) shared repertoire (Mohd and Asmuni, 2016). However, in the Proposal Lab there is a central role for a convenor or tutor for moments of teaching and explanation.

2 The Proposal Lab principles

> **Reading tip**
>
> This chapter is primarily aimed at colleagues supervising a Proposal Lab and programme developers considering introducing such a community of practice. If students are considering a PhD programme that includes a Proposal Lab-like programme, this chapter offers them tools to get a grip on its content and quality.

1 Introduction

1.1 History of the Proposal Lab

Ten years ago, a new development in the organization of doctoral studies took place in the Netherlands, showing many similarities with the UK MPhil programmes and the first two years of an American and Chinese PhD trajectory.

In 1992, Bowen and Rudenstine had already pointed to a problem that arises for many students during the transition from, on the one hand, the highly programmed parts of an MPhil or Master's programme and the first two years of a PhD programme, and on the other, the sudden challenge of having to develop their own research idea: 'A still more troublesome problem, and one mentioned more often than any other hurdle, is selecting an appropriate topic for a doctoral thesis' (Bowen and Rudenstine, 1992: 254). They conclude with an important recommendation which is still as topical today given the still-existing problem of early attrition: 'We suggest seeking ways to encourage students to begin to engage the reality of serious thesis-related research during their first and second years' (ibid.: 283). In this way, the transition from coursework to the preparation of one's own research becomes less abrupt.

As already mentioned in the Preface, almost ten years later Barbara Lovitts confirmed this sketch of the situation that is an international phenomenon: 'A few faculty acknowledged the difficulty of making the transition from course taker to independent researcher/scholar. However, very little concrete advice appears to be dispensed about how to make this transition' (Lovitts, 2001: 73).

To facilitate this transition is exactly what I am aiming for with this handbook. It will be of value to individual supervisors as well as to those university departments that opt for support via Proposal Labs or Proposal Workshops, both belonging to the recently emerged communities of practice.

The development of the Proposal Lab was part of the renewal of the Dutch Research Master's programmes, aimed at supervising and supporting the writing of a PhD proposal. I have been teaching this programme for five years. For both the department and future supervisors, this programme has the great advantage that the prospective PhD candidates are working for months on a PhD proposal that was not a try-out but became the basis of an often successful PhD trajectory, being also part of the material presented during the application for a PhD position.

If we want our PhD candidates to obtain their PhD in 4 years, they must get off to a flying start. This means that they must be able to present the first version of a detailed proposal upon admission to the doctoral programme, and not a quasi-proposal of five hundred words in an embryonic state. That also means that we must make the students work on that proposal in the previous programme. In doing so, they need our information and support. The sudden genius PhD candidate does not exist, and within the context of a Proposal Lab, I do not assume the presence of an individual supervisor from the very beginning. The search for the best supervisor for their project is part of the proposal preparation.

This handbook aims to make this approach to the preparation of a PhD research accessible to the colleagues, in any discipline whatsoever. They will be given the opportunity to offer a Proposal Lab or individual guidance, without having to reinvent the wheel. The guide provides them with several ingredients for their own version: reading suggestions, tools, assignments, etc. They will adapt their version to the specific requirements of their own institute and discipline. However, maintaining the core elements will ensure that the admission of future PhD candidates will be built on a much stronger foundation.

The Proposal Lab is designed to provide faculty guidance and peer support for the development of (1) an elaborated research proposal as a stand-alone exercise, or (2) the basic material for an application for a PhD position or a research position outside academia.

In parallel to the Proposal Lab, students will co-operate intensely with members of the faculty, research group or graduate school, who are experts on their topic. The Proposal Lab is not a substitute for specialized training in particular disciplinary topics, which may be expected from teachers in domain courses and potential future supervisors.

1.2 The Proposal Lab in view of the admission of doctoral candidates

In 1988, the Netherlands started the system of research schools, later converted into graduate schools. I was the managing director of one of the first research schools for a long time. An important part of my work was supporting the selection of new PhD candidates. My colleagues and I put a lot of emphasis on the selection procedure. Writing a rudimentary form of a PhD proposal was an important part of that. However, we agreed that we could only get a good picture of the qualities of a PhD candidate at the end of the first year. The eventual paper had to show whether we had made the right decision and whether the candidate could successfully complete the process.

It soon became clear that this assessment – later called the 'go/no go decision' – did not lead easily to a decision about whether to continue participation in the doctoral training programme. In several cases we did not dare to send out weakly performing candidates. The supervisor often turned out to be more positive and the colleagues gave in to the supervisor's strong plea to continue the candidate's PhD trajectory.

At that time, we were making two kinds of errors in the decision process. We could send a candidate away while the candidate turned out to be a successful PhD recipient somewhere else. Or we could let a candidate pass who eventually did not make it, often after years of struggling. In general, we preferred the second category of mistakes. In other words, we preferred a slowly extinguishing project rather than intervening with a firm hand in a situation where an early termination of the project would have been a defensible step.

This led, again, to more attention on the selection of the candidates. How could we do that better? The committees proposed we were stricter while the procedure was not changed much. Repeatedly, it became clear how difficult it is to get a good picture of the qualities of the candidate based on an admission request, a CV, a rudimentary form of a proposal and an interview of, say, one hour. In particular, the psychological qualities that are necessary for a PhD trajectory can hardly be seen in this way.

While this struggle continued, new developments took place in the Netherlands. In several study programmes, a 2 year Research Master's programme was started. Part of this was in some cases a component in which students were supervised in writing a PhD proposal. In the Faculty of Law of the University of Tilburg, I was involved for 5 years in the teaching of such a programme, together with full professors in law.

More than one hundred students from the Netherlands and Belgium successfully completed this programme and very many of them applied for a PhD position. Very often with success. For the faculty and future supervisors, this programme had the great advantage that the prospective PhD candidates had been working for some time on a PhD proposal that was not a try-out but became the basis for an often successful PhD trajectory.

In 2016, I concluded that the best way to get an idea of the candidate is to see him or her work in a pre-PhD trajectory. In that way, we can evaluate the candidate's familiarity with the literature and the ability to search for relevant publications. We will see initiative in contrast to playing a waiting game. We can check the ability to plan one's work and to comply with deadlines. We see whether the candidate possesses writing skills and knowledge of the necessary methods of data collection and processing. Self-selection is an important aspect of this approach. Several candidates will conclude a PhD trajectory is not an attractive option for them.

The introduction to potential supervisors and their support in writing the proposal are also an integral part of the programme. This has the great advantage that the candidate and the supervisors know exactly what they are about when a final decision must be made on starting the PhD trajectory.

In this guide we concentrate on writing a proposal in the context of a workshop or lab. The emphasis is on the pre-PhD research phase, for example, by way of a special track in the Master's programme, an MPhil programme or the first two years of a US or Chinese doctoral programme. With modifications, the model can also be used as part of the first year of a PhD programme if PhD candidates still have a lot of space to bring in their own research ideas.

1.3 The Proposal Lab in view of graduate student attrition

In her book, *Leaving the Ivory Tower*, Barbara Lovitts raised the issue of graduate student attrition (Lovitts, 2001). In the USA, this is a big problem. The premature departure from the doctoral programmes is also a fundamental problem in the UK. Barbara Lovitts cites three types of costs involved: (1) the costs for the faculty, the department and the graduate school; (2) the costs for the university and society; and (3) of course, the costs for the early leavers themselves who started a project they did not finish. In the world of internationalization of doctoral studies, we can also mention the international subsidy providers being affected badly in the case of thesis projects that ended prematurely.

A lot of research is being done into the reasons for attrition. This is not the place for an extensive literature review. In this handbook, I limit myself to my own research experiences. A crucial point is repeatedly the insufficient preparation for a new study stage and the underestimation of the problems of transition:

- I first discovered this theme in my research on Master's thesis histories in 1980. In several respects, the thesis formed a starting point within a study that had been going on for years and for which people had been insufficiently prepared.
- In the late 1980s, I performed an analysis of the supervisor evaluations of my graduate school's PhD candidates. The students had been working on their PhD for 8 months, which they had been admitted to on the basis of a rudimentary research idea. Their work was assessed by their own supervisor and several other colleagues. The judgements were overly critical and focused on, for example, the literature review, the methodology and research design, problem definition, planning, the limitation of the research ambitions and the lack of working hypotheses or an individual position. These are

exactly the components that are central to the Proposal Lab. By the end of that programme, the participants in the Proposal Lab are more advanced than first-year PhD candidates who come in with a rudimentary research idea and are dependent on a single supervisor.

- In a 2008 study into the quality of PhD supervision, I noted that PhD candidates receive insufficient support regarding the research design.
- In 2015, I interviewed seriously delayed PhD candidates in Law. An important aspect of the substantive problems consisted of postponing major decisions regarding the content of the dissertation together with or despite the supervisor. The overarching theme is that of procrastination. In the case of severely delayed candidates, I came across missing leading research questions and a delayed theoretical perspective. After years of work, clearly formulated research questions could still be lacking. 'I have a topic, but no leading question' said one of the PhD candidates interviewed. Often, their research also lacked focus by not formulating a thesis, a claim, a working hypothesis or a leading argument. Postponing key decisions about the dissertation for years and years compounds all these issues.

An argument in our defence could be that solving the problems is up to our PhD candidates. How could we have foreseen that they would not live up to our expectations raised during the admission procedure? There is only one answer to this: our admission procedures are insufficient. And the most important remedy is to provide a preparatory trajectory that supports candidates in drafting a research proposal and offers them and their supervisors the opportunity to explore the collaboration and each other's strengths and weaknesses.

1.4 Core goals of the Proposal Lab

Our handbook does not have to start from scratch, we are standing on the shoulders of highly regarded colleagues who have covered the important building blocks of our programme. We can integrate much of their work into a process-based didactic of the proposal development. What are my points of departure?

- Supporting the proposal development is one of the most difficult didactic tasks in university curricula. We must advise and assist students without taking over their project. It is their plan.
- Regarding the proposal and the thesis in general, there are all kinds of implicit quality expectations. We must make these explicit as early as possible.
- We often expect students to have study skills that are essential for a proposal. We should not tacitly assume them, but at least we should check them.
- If PhD candidates are dissatisfied with a component of the supervision, in nine out of ten cases this is the lack of attention to the planning. Learning to plan a proposal and subsequent thesis research will change their life.

- Developing a proposal has predictable crisis moments. We can make them explicit and, thus, manageable in our didactics.

The process-oriented nature of my programme is one of its most important characteristics. Tongue in cheek, I once presented the development of a research proposal as a mountain tour, taking us past the Expectations Swamps, Mount Supervision, Lake Independence, Dark Parks and Alleys ... and sketching the qualities that the travel companions must bring or develop.

2 Some didactic considerations

2.1 Foundation in proven didactic insights

In 1986, Mirande wrote his thesis: 'The student as a novice researcher. On the development of educational tools for teachers and students in higher education'. He reports on an educational experiment in which beginning student researchers were supported in a course format in developing a thesis annex research plan.

The model developed by Mirande did not come out of the blue. Important sources of inspiration were earlier experiments developed in the USA. Mirande distinguishes the following models:

1. *The Clinic.* Teacher and participant together analyse the situation of the participant, determine the strengths and weaknesses, and develop an improvement strategy. This could be an interesting model for PhD candidates who are just about to submit a research proposal and who are discussing a penultimate version. The question is whether such a model makes sense if the student has already developed a strong relationship with a supervisor.
2. *The mini-course.* Participants read a handbook in which, for example, the ins and outs of a proposal and the way there are described. They are shown examples of proposals, after which they use a checklist to assess whether their proposal meets the requirements and indicates what still needs to be done. This model also assumes participants who are already well on their way.
3. *The Laboratory.* In this model, the participants are faced with a multitude of learning activities, such as 'learning by doing' and 'learning by discovery', different sources of feedback, 'experiencing self-confrontation' and confrontation with a lab convener, (potential) supervisor and peers.
4. *The tools of the trade.* As a fourth model, Mirande mentions the tools of the trade, a programme in which participants become familiar with rules, checklists, tests, procedures and flowcharts that participants can effectively adapt to their specific goal: their proposal.

Mirande translated important elements of these approaches into a programme for students who are in the first phase of making a thesis plan. Preliminary research showed that their problems centre around the following (Mirande 1986: 85):

- problems with choosing a topic;
- difficulty in formulating the problem;
- problems with the selection of data and ideas to be processed to arrive at a solution to the research questions;
- problems with presenting the research ideas (difficulty with composition or writing);
- self-management problems.

We can compare these topics with our students' own self-evaluation of qualities. In the very first development stage of my programme, they mentioned the following points in individual conversations:

- misunderstandings as regards whether a certain type of research or specific topic would be acceptable;
- finding a well-defined subject and key question; this was mentioned as their main problem;
- differences between the students regarding the familiarity with a subject;
- weak management qualities;
- difficulties in bringing order to thoughts;
- difficulties with focus, topic, main question;
- perfectionism;
- doubts about having control over the study matter;
- worries about qualities of judgement;
- existential doubts about research qualities.

To conclude, my model – the Proposal Lab – meets the following criteria as sketched by Mirande.

1 It is applicable to the writing of a proposal in various disciplines. However, an important feature of my programme is the insertion of discipline-specific knowledge. I therefore advocate a Proposal Lab in a specific discipline.
2 The Proposal Lab is applicable to a wide variety of research topics.
3 It makes explicit and debates the feelings of uncertainty and problems of motivation.
4 It makes explicit and tests the skills that are indispensable when writing a PhD proposal.

In this student-focused Proposal Lab, you will recognize important building blocks from American didactic programmes mentioned above:

- the entrance interview, the final interview;
- skills training;
- reading literature and guidelines (about writing a proposal, searching for literature, writing a review, interviewing experts, planning the proposal and doctoral research, the requirements set for a proposal and the assessment criteria);
- assignments regarding all these skills: learning by doing;
- the study of proposal examples;
- presenting work in progress to peers and (potential) supervisors;
- getting feedback on submitted work;
- writing a first draft proposal – revision – completion with a detailed proposal, a final version;
- peer support and feedback.

This Proposal Lab is also part of a global development of support programmes for (prospective) PhD candidates, all aimed at reducing their isolation and introducing the support of peers and experts other than their own supervisor. For example, they appear under such titles as Doctoral Support Center in the USA or Doctoral Support Groups in the EU.

2.2 Didactic principles and efficiency

Apart from this scientific basis, there is also the aspect of efficiency if we locate such a programme in an MPhil, a Research Master's programme or the first two years of an American PhD trajectory.

In our programme, let us say 20 students, we provide introductions to the following components:

- from topic to question;
- types of questions;
- searching and critically appraising the literature;
- writing a literature review;
- interviewing experts and potential supervisors;
- the role of theory, hypotheses and claims;
- originality of the proposed topic;
- the fundamentals of a proposal;
- the quality criteria that will apply.

The programme also includes assignments and the convener's feedback on the students' products, as well as peer-to-peer comments on work in progress. In a course format (20 participants), the teacher will spend around 9 hours per student.

If we fully individualize the guidance to a proposal (one supervisor per student), this will cost the staff member about 18–30 hours for checking or explaining skills, the preparation of feedback, explaining quality criteria that will be at stake and the meetings with the student, in the months of the proposal development.

Note that the Proposal Lab does not come at the expense of looking for and working with potential supervisors. Their role is also essential in the development of the plan but can be limited to individual conversations in which products resulting from the Proposal Lab will be discussed. Thus, it does not release the prospective PhD candidate's (potential) supervisor from a role in this journey towards a proposal.

Researchers will also be present at important moments to integrate knowledge from the scientific field in which the programme functions into the Proposal Lab. For example, consider the sessions on theory and research design.

2.3 Didactics in practice

1. Deliberately plan a stage of Topic Exploration, to distinguish it from the stage in which developing a research design and research proposal is central.
2. Do focus on the product of the Proposal Lab: the proposal. Choose a proposal format that matches local standards. Very often, the model for a subsidy application with a national science organization works well. If possible, make use of the format used within the local graduate school.
3. Be aware that the participants can and will choose different follow-up programmes. Some will apply for a PhD position, in your faculty or outside. Others will conclude that they do not want to start a doctoral research project but are interested in other types of research jobs.
4. Do not force participants to choose a topic or a certain supervisor too quickly. Allow participants time to explore different possibilities. Make time for doubt and hesitation, for slowing down. However, make use of the possibilities that deadlines offer. At a certain moment, a participant really has to make decisions.
5. Do not assume that participants have already mastered all the basic skills. Be aware that students sometimes have difficulty in admitting that they cannot or do not know something yet. University bluff, i.e. pretending you understand or can do something at university, when you don't, can be a problem. See also independence not as a matter of course. In the case of international students, cultural differences in the relationship between supervisor and student deserve special attention.
6. Work from a didactics of independence. The application of what you instruct the students is central. Learning by discovery!
7. Avoid endless lecturing. If you are introducing a topic, use a maximum of 20 minutes for it. And then ... to work!
8. We can also sabotage creativity and independence, for example, through emphasis on methods or endlessly reading what others have done before.

An impersonal relationship with students will hinder their expression of concerns or uncertainties, and staying on high abstraction levels and offering no time for reflection, re-consideration and making mistakes in the case of genuinely innovative ideas also is detrimental.

9 Think in terms of a laboratory, an atelier, in which the students can observe how their colleagues work. Use peer review and collaboration. They learn a lot from their peers' feedback. Find a balance between the individual and the collective. Before they can do it themselves, young researchers are perfectly capable of assessing the weaknesses and strengths of the work of a colleague.

10 Make the students aware of the great value of asking questions. Always think in terms of questions: 'What questions do I ask of the literature and experts to be interviewed; which questions are central to my presentations of my research (oral and written); what is the guiding question in my research proposal and how does it differentiate into sub-questions?'

11 An important aspect is the balance between the attention paid to the tasks to be performed and their quality and, on the other hand, the growth of the student as a potential young researcher. Is that not always the same? Can a student show strong development and at the same time deliver products that we assess with a mediocre rating? Yes, that is possible. The art of teaching Research Master's or MPhil students and early PhD candidates is to postpone the impatience in achieving good performance. We do well to assess the first two assignments in terms of a learning curve that the student is experiencing. Let us not forget that many participants have never done independent research before. It makes little sense to compare the performance of the first two assignments with a set of criteria that we apply to the products that are submitted in the final phase, in particular, the Final Proposal. Keep in mind, however, that the judgement about the product of the programme should never come as a surprise. In the context of a formative assessment of the interim products, the student must obtain clarity regarding the criteria used as regards the proposal and how the student is doing in that respect.

12 The Research Master's, the MPhil programme and the first two years of an American or Chinese PhD trajectory are a testing phase. We do not know, even if we select well, whether the admitted students have had basic training in fundamental research at PhD thesis level. We will determine this during this Proposal Lab and that may even mean that a practice is created in which students work at different quality levels. When assessing the Final Proposals, the entire group comes together, and the qualities of the documents are judged by the same yardstick. Then, we can issue well-founded advice on a future research career. It is impossible and undesirable to use the first months in which students formulate their interests, topic and questions as the basis for an implicit goodbye to students who disappoint us and for a decision that we will not invest any more in them.

13 The essential tension. The participant in the lab will receive advice from several sides. In the beginning, there is only the lab convener. One of the

aims of the programme is that the participant chooses a supervisor. In some cases, it is clear from the beginning who will be the supervisor. Certainly, if the lab teacher is working in the same field as the supervisor, this can lead to explicit views of the lab convener regarding the content of the research being at odds with the direction preferred by the supervisor. Powerful participants can manage this tension. Other participants may be tempted to want to please all the parties involved. That does not always work. Evaluations show that both participants and supervisors can experience an 'essential tension' between lab convener and supervisors. The lab conveners must be aware of this and become modest in their substantive suggestions as soon as they register that participant and supervisor have found each other.

14 Planning. Repeatedly PhD candidates cite the support in managing the research project as one of the weakest aspects of the supervision they receive. That is a global phenomenon. Learning to plan a research project is one of the most important parts of the Proposal Lab to strengthen their skills in this area. The planning of a 4 year research project will be a major part of the proposal they develop. They must make it us believe it is plausible that it will work in, say, 4 years. They practise this skill in the Proposal Lab itself. They must submit a proposal in about 7–9 months. Planning all activities is essential for this.

3 Proposal Lab objectives

3.1 Generic objectives

The Proposal Lab will deal with the following topics:

- the development of a solid research design;
- individual research skills;
- the formulation of a research proposal;
- an introduction to research strategies and methods of data collection (in that way functioning as an entry point to the detailed study of specific methods);
- teaching the participants how to manage themselves and the (potential) supervisor;
- teaching the participants to critically reflect on their own work and to assess the scientific quality of scholarly publications.

3.2 Objectives in detail

We distinguish three major building blocks in the programme: knowledge, skills and application, all combined with feedback. In the overview that follows, you will find the specifics of each building block.

Objective 1: Knowledge of ...

1 The newest developments in the discipline.
2 The function of theory in scientific research.
3 The function of the research question and the diverse types of research questions.
4 The components of a research proposal and the elements of a research design.
5 The criteria that are used in the evaluation of research designs and research proposals.

Objective 2: Skills such as ...

1 Basic ingredients of intellectual craftmanship.
2 Interviewing experts.
3 Searching for the most important literature.
4 Critically appraising the literature.
5 Writing a literature review.
6 Finding a research niche for starting a new project.
7 Extrapolation: reflecting on one's own research interests and research experiences to make new research-driven choices.
8 Assembling the research questions, finding the required data to answer the question and methods to collect the necessary data.
9 Reporting and communicating with respect to one's own research.
10 Giving and handling feedback (by course teachers, mentors/supervisors and peers).
11 Complying with deadlines.

Objective 3: Application and synthesis

1 Application of knowledge and skills in the development of one's own research plans.
2 Synthesis by putting together knowledge and skills in the development of a research proposal.

4 Admission to the programme

4.1 Information to be given by potential participants

There are many diverse ways in which students can decide that they want to participate in our Proposal Lab. In the first place, the Proposal Lab can be part of an MA programme that prepares students for a research career, outside or within the academic world. Their admission to the Proposal Lab will not be arranged separately but is integrated into the overarching admission procedure.

But let us assume that we offer a Proposal Lab that is not embedded in a study programme that is subject to a serious admission procedure and that is not part of a first-year PhD programme. In this case, it is sensible that the conveners of the Proposal Lab assure themselves of the motivation and some basic qualifications of the person who wants to participate. In the box we see an example of the information the applicant should offer.

Anyway, do not confine yourself to a blind acceptance of everyone who registers! Get a feeling for the motivation and preparedness of your future student by inviting the student to fill in the Snapshot.

> Information to be given by an applicant for your programme:
>
> a. Personal details (name, age, nationality)
> b. Details of previous and current higher education
> c. Prior education in English language (very often these types of programmes will be offered in English)
> d. How did you hear about this Proposal Lab?
> e. The Snapshot (see below)
> f. Curriculum Vitae

4.2 Snapshot assignment

What does this Snapshot look like? We have always used a form that asks for information about the candidate's research interest and topic(s) under consideration, with a maximum of 1,000 words (see Appendix D). The candidates are invited to present information about the origin of their interest in doing research, their prior research experiences, their personal and intellectual qualities that are to their entire satisfaction, where they encountered their greatest problems and what has been the central question they have tried to answer in their most important prior research project.

In the next section of the form, we ask questions regarding 'The way to a new research project':

1 What is your research about?
2 How much is already known about your topic(s)?
3 Why is this research interesting for you and others?
4 Have you already discussed you research interests and topics with others? What were their questions and suggestions?'

The candidate is triggered from this very first moment into thinking about research interests and possibilities. It is unlikely that this will be the foundation for a definitive choice of a subject. What we are investigating is whether the candidate is already able to think about this exciting journey as a beginning researcher.

4.3 Interviewing potential participants

An answer to questions such as given above is an excellent starting point for an interview with the candidate. Other questions that can be asked are, for example:

- Can you summarize the core of your motivation for following our programme?
- Does the possibility of getting a PhD play a role in this?
- Have you ever read a thesis in the discipline of ....?
- If you had to explain to a first-year Bachelor's student what the most important characteristics of a research project in the discipline of ... are, which points would you mention?
- In the research in your discipline, how do you see the relationship between, on the one hand, wanting to understand and explain something and, on the other, solving something?
- What is the best investigation report in your discipline you have read?

Even if you are not in the position or not wanting to deny a candidate the opportunity to participate, then all this information from the candidates is extremely valuable for the fine-tuning of the Proposal Lab. Moreover, the candidates know immediately from which angle the wind blows.

5 The prospectus, the journey and the calendar

5.1 The prospectus

Our assumption is not that students who are considering a PhD trajectory already know what a PhD proposal looks like. We also do not assume that all of them already possess the study skills that they need to achieve a good proposal. This involves finding the important literature, being able to critically evaluate a text, writing a literature review, being able to interview experts about a PhD subject and, finally, drafting a research proposal. We have made this explanation of our expectations into an important goal of the Proposal Lab prospectus. We even try to make explicit the assessment criteria that the participants will have to deal with.

This explanation is particularly important for participants in the Proposal Lab who come from other academic institutions and cultures. They are not yet familiar with the local practices and cannot rely on knowledge of the implicit rules of the game. For example, think of international candidates having been trained in a completely different academic culture.

A good Proposal Lab prospectus gives information about the lecturers, the Proposal Lab prerequisites, an overview of Proposal Lab objectives, the Proposal Lab requirements, the books to be bought, an overview of assignments to be graded and their evaluation criteria, and the evaluation criteria as regards the Proposal Halfway and the Final Proposal.

In Appendix B, you will find a layout for a Proposal Lab prospectus. This layout serves as an example, to be adjusted to your own situation. But try to stick to the level of explicitness and detail that we propose.

5.2 A visualization of the journey

Similar to a real travel guide, we offer our travellers an overview through a real map (Figure 2.1).

Figure 2.1 The map of the journey to a proposal

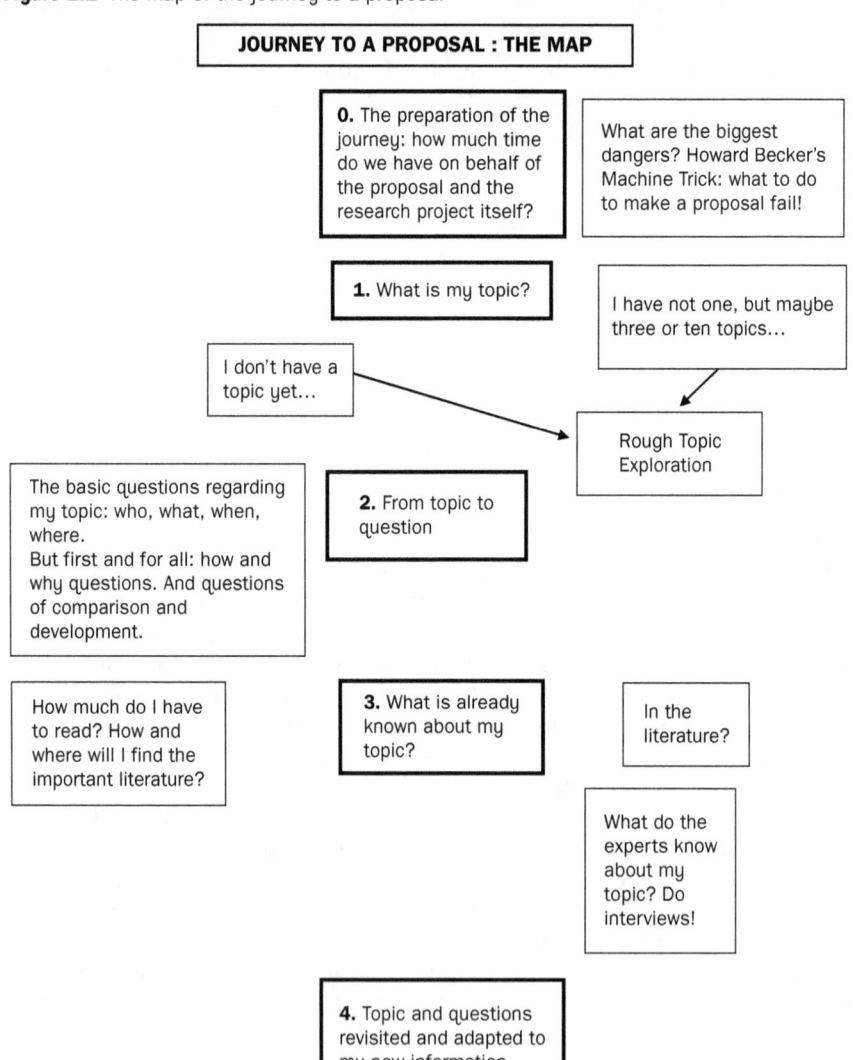

Figure 2.1 (Continued)

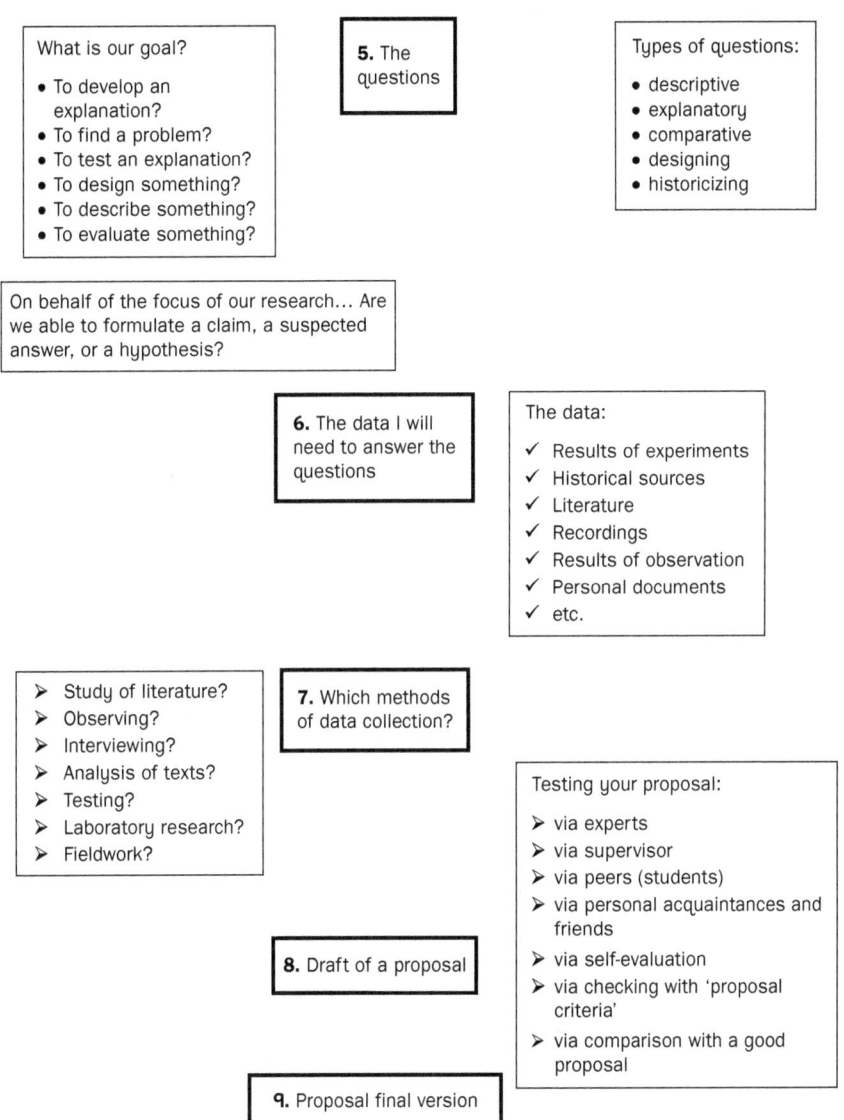

5.3 The calendar

Below is presented a summary of the Proposal Lab sessions, the assignments and individual feedback meetings. To illustrate this, we assume a programme that runs from September to June the following year. You can adapt this to your local circumstances. What must be avoided is haste. A programme of at least

6 months is a workable alternative, with the components staying the same. The components of the programme consist of group meetings, assignments to be made individually and face-to-face feedback discussions with the Proposal Lab convener, (potential) supervisors, experts, and peers.

The programme includes contributions by experienced researchers in conducting research in specific disciplines. For example, they focus on the different possibilities of data collection, current trends in their discipline's research, urgent issues that require research, the role of theory, etc.

The support for writing the proposal is in the hands of one or two experienced PhDs. For the introductions to substantive aspects of the research, the Proposal Lab conveners can appeal to colleagues from their own faculty or research group.

As an example, the calendar in Table 2.1 assumes that the programme starts in September and will take approximately 8 months. Of course, you may adapt this to your own situation.

Table 2.1 Timetable for PhD proposal

	Topic	Time
Before start of the Lab	Pre-orientation on possible topics by participants by filling in the Snapshot	

Topic Orientation Stage	1. Introduction round teachers and students
	2. Your introductions:
	  a Preparing Research: in search of your research topic
	  b The Bigger Picture: Research design and Research Proposal
	3. In class Rough Topic Exploration
		Session 1, third week of September

	Individual feedback on Snapshot + Rough Topic Exploration	First week of October
	a Introduction to diverse types of research in the discipline [X]: the tricks of the trade b Interviewing experts and informants with practical experiences; preparing contacting possible mentors/supervisors c Planning your trip to a proposal	Session 2, third week of October

(Continued)

Table 2.1 (Continued)

Topic	Time
The ins and outs of a research proposal Quality criteria that will apply originality and relevance	Session 3, first week of November
Training in literature search Literature search practicum The importance of embedding in the existing literature	Session 4, third week of November
On the way to a literature review Note-taking and critically appraising reports and documents Writing a literature review	Session 5, fourth week of November
Handing in 'A well-reasoned topic choice'	Second week of December
Individual feedback sessions on 'Well-reasoned topic choice'	Third week of December
From topic to questions The Question Practicum	Session 6, second week of December
Handing in: 1. Literature review 2. Critical appraisal of literature 3. Research question and embedding report	Second week of January
Handing in: 1. Report on literature search 2. Interview report	March 1
Theory, hypothesis and claims Different views on theory The role of propositions The ultimate focus: formulating claims	Session 7, third week of January
The research design Fundamental criteria: validity, reliability What data do we need? How will we collect them?	Session 8, second week of February

(Continued)

Table 2.1 (Continued)

	Topic	Time
Proposal stage	After this last session, the students will work individually on their proposal for some time. It is worth considering organizing a meeting halfway through this period in which the students can present their developing ideas to each other and to you for interim feedback.	
	Handing in Proposal Halfway	1 May
	Individual feedback Proposal Halfway	Second week of May
	Handing in Proposal Final Version	15 June
	Grading of Final Proposal	22 June

6 The literature

Which literature is an essential part of our programme? As mentioned, we do have the books about the characteristics of a research proposal and the books with tips and tricks for the PhD candidates who are facing that challenge. This means that our handbook does not have to start from scratch, we are standing on the shoulders of highly regarded colleagues. We integrate much of their work into a process-based didactic of the proposal development. See Appendix A for detailed literature tips.

3 The journey to the PhD proposal
The students' perspective

> **Reading tip**
>
> In the first place, this chapter is intended for both students and early PhD candidates preparing a proposal within the context of a Proposal Lab or community of practice, as well as candidates who do this on their own with the support of a supervisor. Supervisors can take note of the advice that advanced PhD students give to those beginners, and the advice of supervisors to colleagues who are supervising proposal writers.

1 Introduction: roadmap for the readers

This chapter focuses on the journey to a proposal seen from your position, the proposal writer, the student, or early PhD candidate.

A proposal is not something that we naturally know what it looks like or how to write one. Aspiring PhD candidates are always told: prepare a PhD proposal. However, it is never explained which path will lead to that proposal. Websites, books on supervision and teaching in preparatory university programmes make do with a one-page information sheet on the components of a proposal. For the rest, dear students, find out for yourself!

In this chapter I describe the journey to a proposal as a travel guide. A travel guide is intended to inform travellers about the best preparation, the stages, the must-see attractions, the composition of the travel group and any complications that may arise.

Although the emphasis in this handbook is on the Proposal Lab, we broaden the perspective here. After all, there are other paths that will lead to a PhD project. The structure of this chapter is as follows.

I start this chapter in Section 2 with an important distinction, that between the students or PhD candidates who are allowed to choose their own topic, and those who are going to do research based on a plan developed by a supervisor.

There is another important distinction, that between the different types of PhD candidates in terms of timing their doctoral project. Are we going to do a PhD research, immediately following a Master's programme, or later, for example, in combination with a job? And of course, there is another big difference, namely between the (potential) PhD candidates who come from outside and those who have been taught in this research environment for years. The latter have already mastered the implicit rules of the game. Those coming from outside still must get a grip on that.

Thereafter, I will describe the journey to a proposal similar to following a travel guide (Sections 3–9). The following matters will be discussed:

1 *The map* – a visual overview of the journey to the proposal. I outline the decision moments and central questions that we must answer.
2 *The timing of the trip* – When is the best time to start a proposal and PhD research?
3 *What do we offer our guides and what do we expect from them?* – This is not a solo trip. Many others will play an important role. What can we expect from them? But we don't come empty-handed. Our supervisors, for example, have a great interest in the success of our trip. A successful PhD trajectory brings them and their research group publications, prestige and – in some countries – money. So, there is a mutual dependence between you and your supervisors.
4 *Solo or group preparation* – When preparing a PhD proposal, we usually think of an individual trajectory. We are working on it under the care of one or more supervisors. More and more universities are starting to think about proposal support with a group character. In this book I use the term Proposal Lab, where sometimes a supervisor is already available, but finding one can also be a central point.
5 *The preconditions for a dissertation project* – Money, time, high quality supervision and a convincing PhD completion record of your department.
6 *The stages of my journey* – Exploration, decisions, draft, testing and grand finale.
7 *Anticipating problems and survival tools* – Experiences of our predecessors, advice from peers, travel guides to read.
8 *What do I know at the end of my proposal journey?* – Is a PhD project something for me? Checking my progress, my strengths and weaknesses. And how about my supervisor's perspective?

2 Different paths lead to a PhD proposal

2.1 Solo or group preparation

Do we start the preparation under the care of a single guide (the supervisor), or do we prefer a group approach, such as the Proposal Lab described in this book? Do we travel solo to the proposal, or do we make optimal use of contact with travel companions and travellers who have already completed the journey to the proposal?

I start with an important distinction, that between the students or PhD candidates who may choose their own topic, and, on the other hand, those who are going to do research based on a plan developed by a supervisor. These starting positions place different kinds of requirements on you as a (future) PhD candidate, while in essence the same qualities and skills are assumed. The destination of the proposal journey differs accordingly. In the case of Master's students, the journey to the proposal is essential to determine whether they want to work on this research for about 4 years. With (early) PhD candidates this is usually already established.

There is another important distinction. Are we going to do PhD research, immediately following a Master's programme, or years later, for example, in combination with a job? Inherent to this are often the preconditions in terms of time. Many PhD candidates work (almost) full-time on their research, in contrast to part-time PhD candidates who take longer for their PhD research and must deal with combining research and demanding work and private responsibilities. So, the key question is: should I start my PhD research immediately after completing my previous education or should I first explore other work options and then start my PhD?

As for the timing of the proposal, there are another two options. Making a proposal can be part of a Master's programme or can take place in the first year of a PhD.

2.2 Preparing your own PhD proposal or executing a supervisor's plan

The overview in Table 3.1 shows the main differences between a plan to be drawn up by you as PhD candidate and the execution of a supervisor's research plan.

2.3 What do these variants have in common?

- *Necessary research skills must be checked* and possibly strengthened. Think of the literature search, taking notes, critically appraising the literature, writing a literature review, knowing the building blocks of a PhD proposal and research design skills in your specific discipline.
- We are fumbling in the dark when *we don't know which quality criteria to consider* when assessing our own proposal or when we need to distinguish the strengths and weaknesses of a plan written by our supervisor.

- In both cases, *knowing your supervisor's expectations and planning* the journey to the proposal or *adjusting a research plan written by the supervisor* are of great importance. Know that supervisors have the same expectations of both types of candidates. And in either case, you and the supervisor need to get to know each other.
- Assessment committees assess all dissertations against *the same criteria*.

Table 3.1 Similarities and differences between PhD candidates with different starting positions

Aspect	PhD candidates are working on their own research plan	Doctoral candidates have been selected to implement a supervisor's plan
Research topic	Doctoral candidates choose a subject based on personal interest. To be checked by supervisors	Topic is fixed to a greater or lesser extent. With a wide scope of definition, PhD candidates will have to clarify and specify
Connection with the literature	Doctoral candidates will map the most important literature based on recognized search strategies. To be checked by supervisors	The research plan, including literature references, was often written a year or more ago. The doctoral candidates will have to investigate whether new, recent studies have now come to light. In that case too, the PhD candidate must be familiar with recognized search strategies
The literature review	Doctoral candidates will have to familiarize themselves with the requirements that are set for a literature review. In every thesis, or part of it, a review of the relevant literature is essential	Doctoral candidates will have to familiarize themselves with the requirements that are set for a literature review. In every thesis, or part of it, a review of the relevant literature is essential
Central research questions and sub-questions	Doctoral candidates must familiarize themselves with the requirements of relevance, transparency and coherence that are placed on a good research question and the sub-questions	Based on this knowledge of these requirements and recent literature search, the doctoral candidates must assess whether the research questions meet the criteria

(Continued)

Table 3.1 (Continued)

Aspect	PhD candidates are working on their own research plan	Doctoral candidates have been selected to implement a supervisor's plan
The data that the research must provide	Doctoral candidates determine what information is needed to answer the research questions. To be checked by supervisors	The supervisor usually has a good picture of the data to be collected. The doctoral students check whether the mentioned data still match the possibly modified research questions and new scientific information.
Methods of data collection	The PhD candidates determine the methods of data collection. To be checked by supervisors	The PhD candidates check whether the methods mentioned in the research plan are (still) adequate
The structure of the thesis and the requirements that it must meet	The PhD candidates present a provisional table of contents and know what requirements are set for, for example, Introduction, Literature Review and Conclusions. To be checked by supervisors	The PhD candidates present a provisional table of contents and know what requirements are set for, for example, Introduction, Literature Review and Conclusions. To be checked by supervisors.
The planning of the investigation	The PhD candidates are primarily responsible for the planning of the research and the interim products. To be checked by supervisors.	If all goes well, the supervisor has made the workable planning. The PhD candidates check whether it makes plausible a timely completion of the thesis

2.4 A third variant: the Proposal Lab

In addition to these individual trajectories, I present the Proposal Lab here. Its organization and content are described in Chapter 4. Much of what follows in this chapter refers to details to introductions, assignments and action summaries in Chapter 4. The information that is used in the Proposal Lab can be directly transferred to the individual trajectories to a PhD Proposal.

In the Proposal Lab (prospective) PhD candidates work on their own PhD proposal, supported and guided by a convener. The biggest difference between the individual trajectory and the Proposal Lab model is that optimal use is made of the mutual peer review options that ensure a less individual and therefore lonely adventure. In addition, supervision is not fixed from the start.

Individual supervisors are also relieved of some of the burden. In the Proposal Lab, participants will be trained to a high level in essential research skills, and they are not dependent on the abilities of an individual supervisor.

In a Proposal Lab, explicit attention is also paid to the planning of the journey to the Proposal. Many PhD candidates are satisfied with the supervision they receive, but they often judge the supervision as suitable for improvement in the area of timing and management of the project. The Proposal Lab provides this.

Please note that the Proposal Lab is not a substitute for individual supervision. The exploration of supervision possibilities is a core component of the Lab, and many of the Lab assignments are of direct use for the collaboration between the student and the (prospective) supervisor.

In the development of the proposal, the role of the supervisor becomes essential. The supervisor is the subject matter expert and will be the guide when it comes to the theories relevant to the student's research, the design of the research and the choice of the appropriate methods of material collection. In a general sense, these topics are covered in the Proposal Lab, but when it comes to the elaboration for the student's own research, the supervisor is the first sparring partner.

A special feature of the Proposal Lab is that in all parts of the proposal it is not assumed that you already know or are able to do something. Time and again it is checked whether you have something under control, or whether more information and practice are needed. Sometimes that won't be the case, and then we can quickly move on to the next part. This checking of research skills prevents us from 'university bluff', i.e. pretending that we understand or can do something at university when we don't.

3 The map: an overview of the journey to the proposal

No journey should be undertaken without a visual overview of the stages, different options and the moments when we can determine whether we are on the right course. In Figure 3.1 you will find a graphical representation of the route to a proposal, including all the intermediate steps.

4 The basics of our journey

4.1 Stages in the development of the research ideas

The one-try, ideal version does not exist. Our proposal in the making has different stages and that also applies to the different parts of it. After an initial study of the literature on your subject, you write a try-out version of a literature review. You will discuss this with the Lab convener, supervisors and peers. You will see if you have mastered this skill, and then will move on to a more finalized version for the proposal.

Figure 3.1 The map of the journey to a proposal

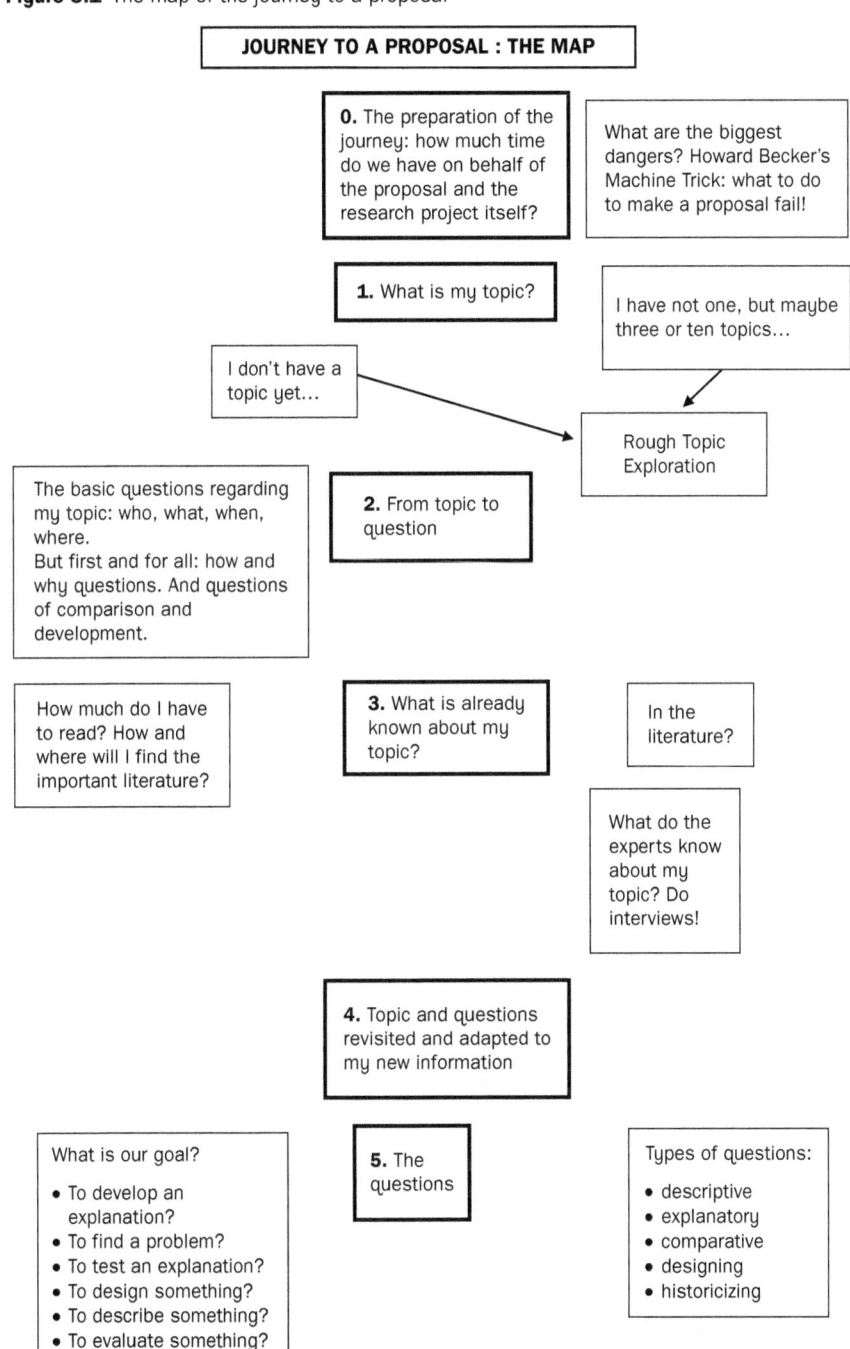

Figure 3.1 Continued

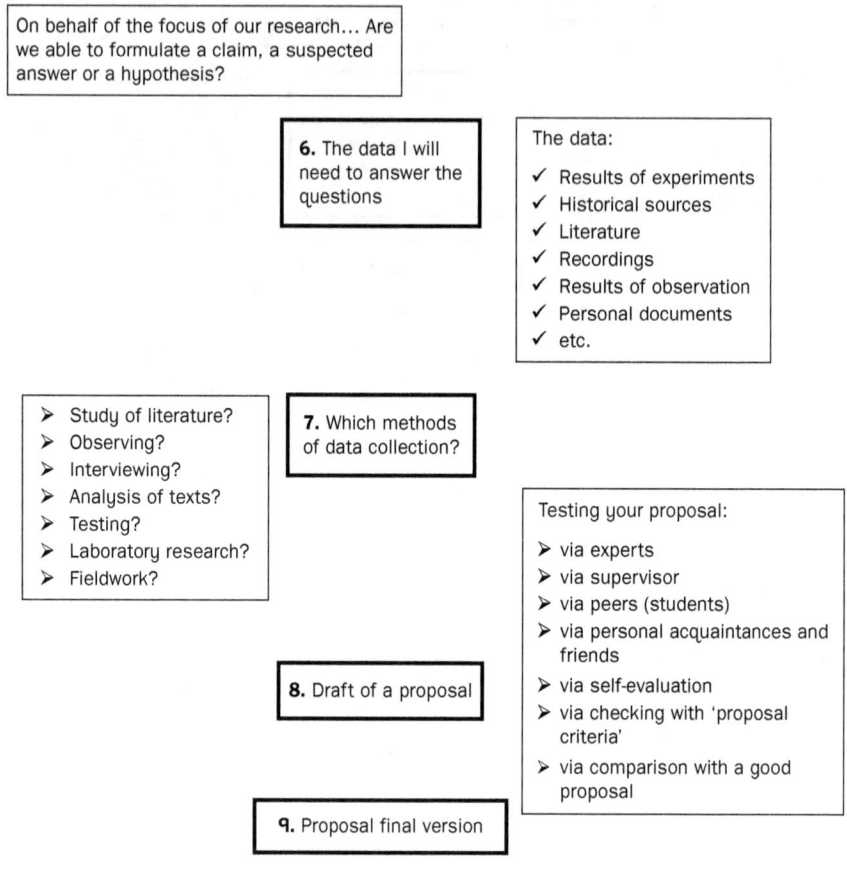

You follow the same procedure for the other components. Think of the research questions. Your first formulation will never be the final version. As you will read more and more, you will adjust your ideas and questions accordingly.

That is why I explicitly refer to a Proposal Halfway in our schedule. You are well on your way and now is the time to present a first draft to the Proposal Lab convener, supervisors and peers.

In the schedule, I distinguish the following key moments:

1 *The exploration*: The exploration of my skills, my interests, the predecessors in this research area, the supervision possibilities and the requirements that are set for a proposal.
2 *The decisions*: My conclusions regarding the subject, the key questions, the material needed to answer the questions and the method of data collection.
3 *The draft*: The Proposal Halfway.

4 *Testing*: Getting feedback from potential supervisors, the Proposal Lab convener, my peers, next to my own assessment of my work, based on the quality criteria I have studied.
5 *The Final*; The final proposal and its discussion with supervisors and Proposal Lab convener.

4.2 Knowing the essentials of a PhD proposal

Early in your proposal journey, you will have to study in detail what the result of your work should look like. In this handbook you will find a lot of information about this. All sections of the proposal are related to the sessions as described in Chapter 4 and in Section 7 of this chapter.

The explanation of the proposal format functions as a map or a compass. The explanation shows the context of everything you are going to learn. It provides you with an insight into the final product and explains why the stages as described in Section 7 of this chapter are necessary when writing the proposal. It may be best to study the proposal composition at an early stage in your project.

Quite often the function of the proposal takes a subordinate position in the handbooks for PhD candidates and their supervisors. The importance of a good proposal is always mentioned, but the road to it is not dealt with in detail. It is quite different in the case of Brewer's (2007) book, *Your PhD Thesis*. Brewer devotes an entire chapter to the research proposal, and this should be mandatory reading. Brewer also makes an interesting suggestion that you can consider. In addition to the proposal, he suggests having an overview submitted of the chapters the student expects to be included in the thesis. This comes close to Umberto Eco's suggestion in Section 7 of this chapter, 'Getting a grip on your main line of argument'.

By making good use of the literature, your supervisor and the information given in Chapter 4, Session 3 and Appendices G and I, you will learn all the details of a PhD proposal. I will summarize the components of a proposal here.

Main components of a proposal

1 Title of the research project
2 *The abstract*: An abstract of a proposal is a collection of statements that comprises the essential points of the document.
3 *The research question*:
   a. Description of the field of study and the existing body of knowledge with reference to that.
   b. The core question. Which central question would you like to answer with the research?
4 *The innovative character of the proposed project*: What is the significance of the proposed research? Does it contain an original contribution to the field of existing knowledge? Is it of specific social or theoretical relevance?

> 5 *Considerations regarding theory and prior empirical research*: Sketch of the *dominant theoretical approaches* and debates. Sketch of the *dominant empirical findings*. How does your research fit in with the present state of research and theoretical discussions in your field? What are the main theoretical concepts you intend to use?
> 6 *Proposition, hypotheses and argument*: What is the central proposition? Your argument? Which are the working hypotheses?
> 7 *The data and methods and design*: In this part of the proposal, you mention the empirical data, the sources and the documents you will use to answer each of the research questions. How do you intend to gather the data? Do you have whatever permissions might be required? Have the necessary informants agreed to co-operate? Do you have access to the sources you need?

Think in terms of proposal stages. Halfway, provide concise and clear answers, based on the ideas and information you have at that moment. If new data and theoretical insights become available, you may have other ideas and your plans may change accordingly. The Proposal Lab convener and supervisors will discuss your Proposal Halfway in a face-to-face meeting. After another two or three months, you will hand in the Final Proposal.

Quality criteria that will apply

Appendix G contains the rubrics that are helpful to get a grip on the criteria that apply to the assessment of a PhD proposal and the result of a PhD trajectory, the thesis. The rubrics as a concept have their origins in the unique work of Barbara Lovitts (2007) whose book is not to be missed: *Making the Implicit Explicit: Creating Performance Expectations for the Dissertation*. If you want to get a grip on the criteria that apply in your discipline, then this book is required reading.

We worked in our Proposal Lab with rubrics such as those developed by Heinze Oost and refined by Rob van Gestel and the author.

The planning of the 4 year dissertation project

In some situations, you are asked to enclose with the proposal a schedule for the 4 years that a PhD project usually takes. The participants in the Proposal Lab or the individual proposal preparers can use two appendices for this purpose. Those are:

- Appendix O: Planning Matrix PhD trajectory (research and other activities).
- Appendix N: Expectations in View of a 4 Year PhD Project. This overview has been composed based on advice by supervisors working in the technical and educational disciplines. It must be adapted to the requirements of your own discipline and field of research. This appendix provides you with a

wonderful starting point for a discussion about the PhD project planning with your own supervisor.

4.3 Your research file

It is wise to keep a 'research file' as you progress. Wright Mills (1970) described this in his 'On intellectual craftmanship'. How can you keep track of determining what really sets you on fire, your previous interests and all the new information you collect? Wright Mills suggests establishing a file on anything that comes to mind about a potential topic and to fill it with random ideas about subjects, newspaper or magazine clippings, notes from scholarly books and articles and snippets of conversations with people. If you're still considering different topics, keep different files. Also write down your enthusiasm for a subject. If you keep such a diary for a few months and write down random ideas about the subjects, you will probably see what fascinates you time and time again and that may possibly become a subject for your thesis. Through a regular re-reading of your notes, literature annotations and interview reports, you will discover lines and patterns, leading to a well-reasoned choice of subject.

4.4 Planning

It is important to undertake good planning for the development of the proposal. We usually only have a limited number of months available. We must allocate our time well and set limits on the time we have available for the various parts of the journey.

First decision: the timing of the trip

When do we start developing a proposal? Do we already do this during a Master's programme or during a PhD programme that has already started? Or, put another way, as an external PhD candidate in combination with a job or major private responsibilities?

No planning is asking for failure

We know everything will fall into the water if we don't plan the trip properly. If it cannot be planned properly, the trip will probably fail. You must not only plan a future PhD trajectory, but also its preparation.

An example of planning

The Gantt chart in Figure 3.2 shows an example of the planning of a PhD proposal. This planning assumes that you also have other (study) activities. If you can work full-time on the proposal, the 8-month period can be reduced.

However, it is important that the period contains sufficient moments of reflection and possibilities for revision of the work in progress.

For a detailed explanation, read the information in Chapter 4, Session 2.

Figure 3.2 Example of a proposal planning (10 months available)

Task	Sept	Oct	Nov	Dec	Jan	Feb	Mar	Apr	May	June
Snapshot	x	x								
Literature search training			x							
Literature search	x	x	x	x	x	x	x			
Literature review				x	x					
Formulating research question, embedded in study of the literature				x	x					
Well-reasoned topic choice			x	x						
Literature search report					x	x				
Interviewing experts and writing interview report		x	x	x		x				
Finding supervisors	x	x	x	x						
Meeting supervisors				x	x	x	x	x	x	
Proposal Halfway						x	x	x		
Final proposal									x	x

> **Action**
>
> Make your own planning chart for a proposal and discuss it with a peer, supervisor and the Proposal Lab convener.

4.5 Getting a grip on the main line of your argument

In 1977, Umberto Eco wrote *Come si fa una tesi di laurea* [How to write a thesis], containing the chapter, 'The table of contents as a working hypothesis'. It is inspiring and structuring to think about the title, the table of contents and an introduction early in the making of a research plan. In this way we force ourselves to think about the broad outline of our project. Umberto Eco defines this very first table of contents as a working hypothesis and sees the draft introduction as the analytical commentary to the table of contents. We can begin to do this as soon as we are well under way in the exploration of the literature and embryonic ideas about our research start to arise in the form of a possible topic and guiding research questions.

Of course, these are not the final versions. Eco says:

> The function of the preliminary introduction ... is that it gives the opportunity to capture your ideas within a framework that will not be changed unless your thesis is going to change completely. In this way you will be able to keep an overview of your trips and raids.
>
> (2005: 137)

Of course, this preliminary introduction will have to be rewritten many times before the thesis is handed in. Once you have conducted an initial literature search, developed a first version of the topic and the research questions, you can see this early table of contents as a well-grounded look into the future. Your supervisor will really appreciate that!

An even more condensed picture of the result is obtained by thinking about our project in terms of a 250-word blurb of our forthcoming dissertation. This exercise really triggers free and courageous thinking about your project. What is the aim of your dissertation? What will this dissertation explain? And what will be its structure and methodology? And why are you so suitable for this research?

4.6 Flexibility: working with research scenarios

There are moments of choice within your project. You may collect the material in one way or another. Access to certain locations or research facilities can be achieved in various ways. Countries, archives or people important to your research may turn out to be inaccessible. It provides relaxation by thinking about parts of our research in terms of options and scenarios. We do not want to detract from our central goals, and we know how our research will ideally progress, but thinking in terms of variants means that we do not panic if something goes wrong.

4.7 Buffer time!

It is very calming if we plan our activities in such a way that we want to finish them before the hard deadline arrives. So, if our proposal must be ready in 8 months, we secretly determine that we will bring the finish forward one or two months. This means that we schedule buffer time in view of serious problems and any delays in our work we might encounter. If we plan our own work exactly in accordance with the deadlines set by others, we immediately feel panic if something goes wrong.

4.8 Maximum use of peer support

When does peer feedback occur in the Proposal Lab and how could you organize this in an individual proposal trajectory? Examples of peer support are:

- In search of your topic. Students interview each other (Session 1, Proposal Lab).
- Discussing 'best practice' PhD proposals of predecessors in subgroups (Session 1).
- Preparing the interview with experts, peers and potential supervisors. We are asking the students to interview each other (Session 2).
- Introduction by a PhD candidate, who previously has attended our programme, presenting experiences with the literature search (Session 4).
- Students will be divided into separate groups to formulate research questions on their research topics (Session 6).
- Some time before the session, students read two proposals written by their predecessors. They must pay attention to the data and methods section in these proposals and evaluate them against the criteria mentioned in Appendix G, 'Criteria for evaluating research questions'. They bring their judgements to the session and discuss them in three sub-groups (Session 9).
- Students are placed in pairs and each one gets 15 minutes to tell their colleague: what the central research question is, what the sub-research questions are, and which (methodological) steps they will take to answer these questions (Session 9).

I give these examples because they can also be easily translated to the situation in which you are working on a proposal on an individual basis. There is a good chance that you will start your work near colleagues who are also working on a proposal. The trick is now to find them and to organize peer support. In essence, this consists of interviewing each other, studying, and discussing the good practices of your predecessors, giving each other feedback, and receiving feedback from colleagues who are more advanced with their PhD research.

4.9 Intervision

A special form of peer support is what we call intervision in the Netherlands. A group of colleagues meets regularly to discuss important issues. The presentation and discussion of one of the matters that one of the colleagues wants to discuss are central. On the next occasion it is someone else's turn. Everything

Table 3.2 Stages in an intervision meeting

Activity	Duration in minutes
Each participant presents a case, an issue	5
The group decides which case or issue will be dealt with today	2
The presenter explains the case or issue and the questions he or she wants to present to the other participants	5
Participants formulate informative questions	20
Presenter may reformulate questions to group	5
The participants discuss the case. The presenter does not participate actively in this part of the meeting. Only listens and makes notes.	15
Each of the participants notes down one piece of advice	2
The participants read their advice notes	2
The presenter reacts. Which bits of advice are interesting? Which concrete steps will be taken?	5–10
Plenary exchange of experiences by the whole group	15

can be discussed, from very practical matters (for example, the unavailability of technical resources) to parts of a proposal that drive someone to despair. The condition is that all participants are motivated to assist their colleagues. An intervision meeting is tightly organized (Table 3.2).

4.10 Action summary

As regards proposal requirements

1 Read Proposal Information and Tips, Appendices G and I.
2 Read Brewer (2007: 79–93) 'The Research Proposal' or another text that deals with the details of a PhD proposal. Write down three to five sentences, maximum, you consider to be of the utmost importance, interest, etc. Explain your choice.
3 Read Watts (2001) 'The Holy Grail. In Pursuit of the Dissertation Proposal' (available at: https://dusk.geo.orst.edu/prosem/PDFs/InPursuitofPhD.pdf). You will find here also a few examples of successful research proposals, and the insights and reflections of the authors on their proposals.
4 Read two proposals, written by your predecessors, and evaluate them on the basis of the information in Proposal Information and Tips, Appendices G and I.
5 Read Chapter 4, Session 3.

As regards planning

1. Read Chapter 4, Session 2 and Section 9.5 in this chapter, 'What is my supervisor's perspective?'
2. Plan the topic choice and the journey to the proposal. Make use of Appendix F: Planning the Well-Reasoned Topic Choice and Proposal Design. Remember to incorporate buffer time and other activities that demand time!

As regards the research file

1. Start your research file from day 1.

As regards peer support

1. If you are developing a proposal on your own, contact peers in a similar position and your predecessors to organize extra feedback.

5 Our guides: the supervisors and the Proposal Lab conveners

Developing a strong relationship with good supervisors is essential, but how do we find them? It is possible that the supervisor and you already know each other well. But especially for Master's students and early PhD candidates coming from outside, a careful exploration of supervisor possibilities is essential.

If you have been accepted as a PhD candidate who has applied for a specific research project, the supervision is often already set.

> Most supervisors have the best of intentions but are not mind readers. Be specific about what you need. You are very likely to get it … You will also need the courage to turn down some requests or to keep probing, if things are unclear.
> (Advice by PhD candidate)

5.1 Interviewing to get feedback and to explore supervision options

Whether you are participating in a Proposal Lab or individually preparing for a dissertation project, interviewing experts is of great value, even in situations where you already have a supervisor.

If you don't have a supervisor yet, one of the aims of your interview is to find out if one or more of these experts are really interested in your project. If there is interest and if there is a click in a more general sense, you can decide for yourself after the interview whether you want to invite them to be your supervisor. It is good to consider this after the interview and not make it a topic of conversation during the interview. Hold your cards close to your chest. Once supervision has been seriously discussed, it is very difficult to return to it. Also you may meet scientists in subsequent interviews whom you would rather have as a supervisor.

In the Proposal Lab, this interviewing of experts is an important part. The primary goal is to get feedback on your research ideas in the making. In Chapter 4, Session 2, you will find numerous tips for preparing professionally for an interview and the quality requirements an interview must meet. See also Appendix L, Section 1.

5.2 What do the supervisors expect from you?

There are several good books that inform you about the do's and don'ts in a relationship between supervisors and PhD candidates. I mention here a classic, *How to Get a PhD*, by Estelle Phillips and Colin Johnson (2022). They discuss the composition of a supervisor team, and the expectations supervisors have regarding their PhD candidates. Among those expectations I mention here: being independent, presenting work that is not just a first draft, regular meetings and being honest when reporting on progress. Do also read the paragraphs on educating your supervisors and how to reduce the communication barriers. Many good suggestions are also made in the Action summary: the plea for a supervisor team (as opposed to working under the supervision of one single supervisor), reducing communication barriers, discussing the working relationship (next to the research content) and setting deadlines.

Earlier, I wrote that PhD candidates are on average positive about the quality of the supervision but have regularly noted a lack of planning and project management on the part of the supervisors. This is where the student who prepares a proposal can really take the lead. Read Chapter 4, Session 2.

PhD candidates have many opportunities to manage the course of their supervision. Think about a proactive role in the planning of the proposal journey and gaining insight into the quality criteria that apply to the components of a proposal. I think being proactive is key here. This means that the student can take the initiative in many areas and thus manage the relationship with the supervisor.

Here are some more operating features of meeting and steering your supervisor's expectations. You will start from a strong position if you know the following:

- what a proposal looks like;
- which quality requirements it must meet;
- how you can organize a 4 year research project;
- how to search the literature, and how to critically appraise it;
- what a literature review looks like;

- how to plan research and its preparation;
- how a dissertation is composed because you have analysed good examples.

And we offer and promote growing independence as evidenced by the following:

- no question by your supervisor without a tentative answer on your part;
- informing yourself about the evaluation criteria regarding your literature search, literature review, research question and proposal;
- pre-evaluating your work before meeting your supervisor;
- recording the meetings with your supervisors and submitting the minutes to them;
- working with multiple supervisors;
- planning your activities without being asked by others to do so;
- making use of peer feedback;
- internalizing an '80 per cent ready model' to avoid procrastination.

I need to clarify that last point. Victoria took part in one of my programmes. A very good participant, but she suffered from the urge for perfectionism. And that led to more and more reading, and more and more drafts before she wanted to hand something in. And that had to be 100 per cent okay. The result was delay. At a certain point we agreed on the '80 per cent ready model'. This meant that she no longer was striving for a result that was 100 per cent okay but was satisfied with work that she felt still needed to be improved ... 80 per cent done. And when she discussed this with her supervisor, she indicated in an accompanying email what she thought still needed to be done. In one case the supervisor agreed with her, in another case he thought the work was fine already. In any case, the result of this was a brake on perfectionism and her procrastination came to an end.

5.3 And what can you expect from your supervisors?

I present two sources of information here, in addition to the experts' knowledge as mentioned above. What expectations can you distil from research and the recommendations of the supervisors themselves?

What the research says

What can you expect from your supervisors? Several times I conducted research among PhD candidates and supervisors. I will not go into all the research results in detail. Here I summarize the main results of a university-wide study at Utrecht University (Sonneveld et al., 2011). What were the PhD candidates satisfied with? Where did they see areas for improvement?

On the basis of my own research, my suspicion is that you can look forward to the (expected) supervision with confidence. You can use the information below to operationalize your own supervision expectations.

Let me start with the overall assessment by the PhD candidates. In general, the PhD candidates are satisfied with the way in which the main supervisor fulfils these tasks (average, 3.7 on a scale of 1 = very dissatisfied, 5 = very satisfied).

Some 89 per cent have at least one meeting per month with the supervisor; 73 per cent have multiple calls per month. People tend to regard this as more than sufficient.

Aspects of the supervision that PhD candidates are satisfied with in decreasing order:

1. Contact, the social side
2. Contact and availability, the quantitative side
3. Interest, enthusiasm and involvement
4. The supervisor's expertise
5. Project and time management
6. Support and supervision
7. Support in writing and publishing
8. Room to manoeuvre
9. Feedback
10. Community building and networking
11. Working conditions
12. Support in preparation of career and long-term perspective
13. Transparency of expectations.

The low position of 'Transparency of expectations' is alarming!

Next to the appreciation, there are also points that could be improved. What do these PhD candidates mention? A total of 543 PhD candidates explained their dissatisfaction in more detail. What were they less satisfied with?

- Contact (the social side)
- Contact and availability (the quantitative aspect)
- Project and time management
- Expertise of the supervisor
- Support and supervision

These Utrecht results are in line with much research among PhD candidates, inside and outside the Netherlands. The supervisors almost always score between 'more than satisfactory' and 'good' in a general assessment of their supervision. And there is always 10 per cent of PhD candidates who are not satisfied. If a university or department on average scores below 7 on a 10-point scale, then there is work to be done.

5.4 What advice do supervisors give?

Also very informative are the tips supervisors give each other. This offers you a glimpse into the supervisors' kitchen. How do they view supporting you on the way to a proposal?

I asked supervisors from TuDelft and the University of Twente to make suggestions to supervisors for good supervision. Their recommendations show that the suggestions of experts such as Phillips and Johnson do not come out of the blue. The recommendations below by supervisors also provide you with a benchmark against which you can test the support and supervision you obtain and suggestions on what to do if things do not go according to plan.

Scouting for talent

> There are three types of candidates. The first of these are former Master's students. Secondly, there are candidates that you met at a conference or during a visit or who have been recommended by a colleague whose judgement you value highly. The third category, which is also the most difficult to judge, are the candidates that you need to assess purely based on written materials.
>
> Previous experiences with a candidate in the Master's programme can prove extremely valuable. In the Master's phase, I teach subjects that many students struggle with. But there are always a few good ones who just love the work and cannot get enough of it. The ones that enjoy it come back for their Master's thesis. If you have supervised someone during graduation for an entire year, you have quite a good idea of someone's strengths and weaknesses and can effectively assess whether you would like to continue with that person for another 4 years. The Master's results provide a good impression of the students' qualities, enabling you to screen them for potential PhD talent, which makes these kinds of candidates the safest bet in my experience.

Dealing with diversity

> The candidates that we get are ready and able to adapt and to be flexible, otherwise they would not have made it to our institute. I sometimes hesitated to bring cultural issues on the table, when I suspected that was hampering communication, but when I did, it worked quite well and really improved the contact.

Supervision flexibility

> My first observation is that there are few general rules which can be applied to PhD supervision, because all heavily depends on the particular candidate. Some PhD candidates want to have their independence and just want to discuss some preliminary results with you, while others need a meeting every

week and you need to point them to every specific issue. Okay, you are right when you think that this is an exaggerated view on the topic. However, it makes clear that a PhD supervisor need to be quite flexible in the way how to approach a candidate.

Let me say something obvious. Do not forget that your PhD candidates are also people: they will have good and bad days. They will need some time to understand what must be done (i.e., to properly define their topic). They will have their own interests and wishes so you should be prepared to accept minor changes in your original research plan. They will have to read a lot and will benefit a lot from informal talks with other staff members (this will help them to sharpen initial PhD project ideas and to decide on the direction that they would like to follow).

Stimulating independence

An important and delightful function of the supervisor is to be the sparring partner of the PhD candidate. Play with arguments, allow, and even encourage your candidate to disagree, provided good arguments can be given. It keeps us sharp. PhD candidates are supposed to become independent researchers, who will be able to guide others in research. That means that they must be allowed space to follow their own opinion, interests, and methods, it is their work, their thesis (within the limit of agreed topic, etc.). This is something to be made clear at the start since some may feel left alone and without direction while one is trying to give them space. As much as possible, let them do what interests them most and what they are good at, then they will do wonderful things. Here, the supervisor comes in to ease the way.

Once the PhD is properly defined, you should slowly give them more responsibility and, for instance, let them decide when they would like to meet you. In these meetings you should always listen to the candidates (who are slowly becoming experts on the topic) and give clear but open advice (i.e., do not push them to go into any predefined direction – unless you see that they are very lost).

From the outset, ensure that there is a reasonable level of structure. The direction you provide should decrease as the PhD candidate makes progress. Some candidates take time to become accustomed to the demands we place on their own initiative. Challenge the PhD candidates by asking questions rather than merely providing answers. They have personal responsibility for honing their research question, compiling their plan, and taking control of the process.

The first stage: the proposal

Many of my recommendations relate to the starting phase of a PhD project, i.e., finding the research topic and writing a research proposal.

The first six months of a PhD candidate are especially important. In my view, you should reserve some extra time for this period. You should meet them often, and make sure that they feel comfortable. I would use these meetings to learn about their background and to listen to their ideas.

Do's

- Help the PhD candidate in defining the scope of the PhD project (during the qualifier phase but also in the ongoing process). What is too much, what is too little to do research on?
- Support the PhD candidate in 'exploring frontiers', to try new things which, at first sight, might look a bit inappropriate.
- Encourage candidates to be creative, to produce ideas that are new, relevant to the research community and which they feel excited about. At the beginning, do not be too focused on the feasibility and the limitations of the research.
- Do advise candidates to do a decent literature study to know what research questions could be 'cutting-edge' research in their field of science.
- Once several research questions are identified, they must be turned into research hypotheses, thereby operationalizing the research question. This requires finding out about appropriate methods, existing data, sampling schemes; hypotheses are often not testable and have to be modified; maybe some research questions must be dropped as necessary data to answer them cannot be collected.
- Explain to candidates the purpose of the introduction and sketching the state of the art in the proposal, i.e., it puts the research into context, documents what previous research has found out and where there are research gaps. The introduction should contain all the aspects necessary to understand the research questions.
- Help candidates to put various research questions into a larger research concept.
- Check proposals for sufficient detail on how to answer research questions, i.e., description of methods, sampling strategy, availability of images and spatial/non-spatial information.

No hiding problems

At the end of a meeting the steps for the coming next at least 3–4 weeks should be clear and then I want to see some results. If something in between went wrong, or the candidate got stuck, I want to be informed, and not hear after 4 weeks that there is no result because of a software problem, for instance.

Attention! The perspectives of students and supervisors may vary.

PhD candidates and supervisors may differ in their evaluation of the quality of supervision. In a survey among PhD candidates and supervisors in the same research institute, I discovered that the PhD candidates rated their supervisors lower than the supervisors rated themselves on the following qualities of supervision (Sonneveld and Scager, 2008):

- up-to-date expertise on the topic of my research;
- providing helpful advice on the research design and methodology;
- helping to maintain a clear focus on the research objectives;
- providing constructive feedback on the work;
- asking questions that make me look at the work from a new perspective.

PhD candidates and supervisors may also think differently about the importance of aspects of the supervision. In my research project, the PhD candidates attached more value to the following parts of the supervision than their supervisors:

- has up-to-date expertise on the topic of my research;
- is available when I need him/her;
- is understanding;
- meets me also at informal occasions;
- makes me feel at ease;
- advocates for my needs and interests;
- allows me to choose my own direction;
- provides guidance that matches my needs;
- inspires me;
- collaborates with me in publicizing (conference papers, articles).

This overview serves to make you aware of the fact that you and your supervisors may think differently about the importance of certain aspects of the supervision and about the quality of the supervision provided. The trick is to organize your communication in such a way that these differences become visible and can be discussed.

6 The preconditions

Apart from the substantive aspects of the preparation of a PhD project, the foundation must also be in order. Consider the following points.

- The time available. How many years will be available for the project? If a project has not already been prepared in detail in a preliminary study phase, do assume 4 years for a full-time project.

- Is it clear what will happen if a PhD candidate runs into time problems due to external causes? Consider, for example, delay caused by technical or visa problems.
- Is the PhD candidate not hindered by other university activities that require much more time than planned? Think of the obligation to provide education that exists here and there.
- Are the finances for the research in order? If the PhD candidate still has to search for funding during the research, there is a very high chance of delay.
- Is there a healthy organization of the supervision? In principle, more than one supervisor is assumed.
- Is the organizational context of good quality? How does your department score in terms of completion rates and time to degree?

7 The stages

7.1 Preparations

Earlier in this chapter, I made some literature suggestions. In addition, look for proposal tips on the internet. A search with the keyword 'PhD proposal' will lead to countless sources where you can get meaningful information.

7.2 Orientation: the topic, the problem you want to study

A good idea and a good plan do not come to us spontaneously but are created by a systematic approach. It all starts with a topic. Three starting positions are conceivable. You already have a clear-cut idea about a subject. Or you find ten different topics interesting. Or you are still walking about completely in the dark. The exploration of possible topics differs depending on this starting situation.

In the first place, I distinguish an exploration that can lead to a confirmation of the subject you are so enthusiastic about. You will investigate the feasibility, the attractiveness (for example, has it been done before?), the supervision options and whether it connects with a research programme in the faculty or research group.

In addition, there is the pure exploration. You have no idea about a subject yet. How do we define such an exploration? It is a broad-ranging, systematic, well-planned search with the aim of discovering a good research topic, leading to a research proposal.

To strip the search for a subject of its mythical aspects, we define the exploration of possible research topics as a research exercise as such. The essentials of a research design apply:

- What is the main *question you want to answer by the exploration?*
- How are your interests *embedded*?

- In your study biography
- In your social interests and activities
- In the literature
- In the intellectual environment.
- *Are you able to explain the relevance of the topic exploration* for you and possible supervisors, in other words, your motivation?
- *Which sources* do you need when deciding on the topic?
- *How will you find these sources?*
- *How will you report on* your well-reasoned topic choice?

Booth et al. (2008) suggest several sources that you may consult and give useful tips. Among them: finding what interests other researchers, skimming the latest issues of journals, asking questions suggested by your sources (think of the concluding discussion paragraph in many journal articles), talking with practitioners, attending lectures, asking instructors about the most contested issues in your field, and finding internet discussion lists in your field.

It may happen that your exploration does not lead to one subject but to seven options. How then to make the final choice? Howard Becker (1986: 54) made a great suggestion:

> Write whatever topic comes into your head, in no more than one or two sentences ... you will see that they share two or three central ideas, which are almost always variations on a common theme that interests you very much.

Practise this type of exercise in an analysis of your own earlier papers and reports to see if there are core elements in your interests.

Various obstacles can arise in this topic exploration: the topic is too broad ... we can't find literature on our topic ... we must broaden the search field ... we can't find a supervisor ... our preferred topic has been done before ...

We can also encounter problems in the personal sphere. Preparing a thesis plan asks for a change of study style. We must shift from a more consumptive study attitude to one where production, daring to rely on intuition and independence are central.

Thus, in this handbook we do not assume that you have already chosen a topic for your research. That is why we have developed a few tools to support you in the exploration of your interests.

7.3 Summary

In the earliest stage of your topic exploration, you may complete the Rough Topic Exploration Matrix (see Appendix E). The matrix mentions several information sources. We ask you to write down which possibilities you are considering for contacting, reading, and analysing. Do not misunderstand this invitation: you are not asked to take a hasty decision about your topic. We only want you to think in a systematic way about the strategies you will use in developing concrete and more specific ideas about a possible research topic.

In the very early stages of your participation in the Proposal Lab or in the initial phase of getting to know an individual supervisor, this Rough Topic Exploration Matrix together with the Snapshot (see Appendix D) provide an excellent basis for brainstorming the next steps. In the Snapshot form you will find the points on which your Lab convener or your individual supervisor would like to hear more from you. For example: Why are you interested in doing research, have you been involved in research before? In your prior research experience, which of your personal and intellectual qualities were to your entire satisfaction? Where did you encounter the greatest problems? Can you tell us something about the topic(s) you have in mind? Why is this research interesting for you?

After a few months of intensive consultation with sources and experts, this exploration is followed by a well-reasoned topic choice (see Appendix H). If you are already sure of your topic, the moment for this well-reasoned topic choice can be brought forward. The well-reasoned topic choice focuses on the approach of the 'topic exploration' and your evaluation of the approach: what went well? Where did you meet problems? How did you solve them?

Thus:

- Read Booth et al. (2016). Move from topics to questions and the information offered in Chapter 4, Session 1 of the Proposal Lab.
- Fill in the Rough Topic Exploration Matrix, the Snapshot and the Well-reasoned topic choice.
- Discuss these documents with: the Proposal Lab convener, individual supervisors and your peers.

7.4 Disciplinary embedding and the literature review

The topic exploration often deals with written sources. Which researchers have made the trip in this area before? What have they written about it? What were their main findings? And what suggestions for research do they make? A good review of these predecessors and their work is important for a good research design. You will become aware of your closest colleagues, get a grip on what is already known and develop a feeling for the hot issues in your research niche. Finding the most important literature is a dialectical process. You will start with an embryonic research interest, will search for the associated literature, and will subsequently adjust or drop the subject, will again search for literature, etc.

In Chapter 4, Sessions 4 and 5 of the Proposal Lab, you will find a lot of information about these essential skills. Below, I summarize the main points. You will get the suggestions in view of what is asked from you in Section 3 of the proposal, to give a 'Description of the field of study, the existing body of knowledge and theoretical perspectives':

- What don't we know and understand? What has been neglected?
- What is the central object of the proposed research? And what is the research objective? Try as hard as you can to formulate your research interests in terms of a conceptual problem, in terms of what we don't know.

- Or in terms of what we don't understand, in terms of something that we want to make understandable for others. Don't focus too early on practical problems, things you want to solve in the practical sense.

This description of the field of study will also enable you to argue the innovative character of your research (Section 4 of the proposal):

- The newsworthiness, theoretical and/or practical or social relevance, and scope of the research problem.
- What is the significance of your thesis? Does it contain an original contribution to the field of existing knowledge? Is it of specific social or theoretical relevance?

7.5 Searching the literature

As preparatory reading, it is wise to read Aveyard (2007), Chapters 1–4. These chapters deal with questions like:

- Why are you doing a literature review?
- How can you determine which literature is important for your project?
- How can you keep a close connection between your research question and the literature search?
- How to search for the literature?

She underlines the importance of having a research question that is neither too big nor too focused on your topic (ibid.: 66). 'Ideally you will retrieve 10–20 references that are well focused on your topic ... it would be difficult to address your research question with fewer references, but you would be inundated with literature if many more references were identified'.

Initially, you will encounter a multitude of articles and books in your literature search. An important aspect of the search is an increasingly sharp focus on the small group of texts and authors that are relevant to your research. Ultimately, you will arrive at the 15–20 texts and authors predicted by Aveyard (2007). Although her book is written from the perspective of health and social care, it is also extremely useful in other fields of science.

Preparatory reading

Do also study the information given in Chapter 4, Session 4 'Searching for the important literature'.

Professional support in searching the literature

If you participate in the Proposal Lab, you will receive an introduction to the different search techniques from librarians and you will also practise search techniques. As an individual PhD candidate, you can investigate whether your university's library offers such training facilities.

The most important aspects of a literature search are:

- having a systematic approach;
- using different methods of searching the literature:
  - electronic searching and searching hard copies of books;
  - additional methods of identifying relevant articles and books, e.g. snowball sampling or scrutinizing reference lists of key articles or authors' names, etc.
- recording the search strategy and writing down the strengths and limitations of the strategy;
- using abstracts to identify the relevance of an article or book.

Starting finding sources

Your university will enable you to search the websites leading to the most important journals in view of your research.

Action

Prepare a brief note (maximum two A4 pages) for your supervisor or Proposal Lab convener containing the following information:

- formulation of your provisional research topic;
- an overview of the journals you would like to consult with respect to your research topic;
- the title of the journals and the motivation for your choice;
- possible problems you have met in this exercise.

Know, for example, French, Spanish and German journals are also an option, or journals from other disciplines. The minimum condition is that the journals are scientific ones!

Action

Open the journal websites and apply the search principles you have been learned or have studied, in combination with the insights you gained by reading the chapters in Aveyard (2007).

The literature review

Many books have been written on the literature review and many internet sites are available.

- I like to use Aveyard (2007), Chapters 6–8 (about synthesizing your findings and presenting your literature review).
- Do also read two chapters in Booth et al. (2016) *The Craft of Research*: Chapter 5, 'From problems to sources' and Chapter 6, 'Engaging the sources'.
- Study Chapter 4, Session 5 of the Proposal Lab (the literature review).

In Chapter 4, Session 5 of the Proposal Lab, you will find detailed information on note-taking regarding sources, the critical appraisal of sources and the essence of a good literature review.

> **Action**
>
> Write down your research area, a specific research theme and your provisional research topic. In this assignment, we ask you to try and fill out a complete 'specification'. Try to follow the specification steps of:
>
> 1. the discipline;
> 2. the disciplinary subfield;
> 3. your theme;
> 4. essential 'others' (fellow researchers);
> 5. their debates;
> 6. the remaining questions (in your view, in the opinion of other authors);
> 7. your niche for doing something relevant and original;
> 8. theoretical anchor points, as offered by other authors;
> 9. your subject.

Quality criteria

In this handbook you will find information about the quality requirements that a literature search, a critical appraisal of the literature and the literature review must meet (Appendix L). The positioning of one's research within the discipline will be evaluated on the basis of its argument for the newsworthiness, theoretical and/or practical or social relevance, and scope of the research problem (originality, relevance).

For the different quality levels at which this positioning can be performed, see Chapter 4, Session 4 and Appendix L, Section 4, 'Evaluation of a literature review'.

> **Action**
>
> Read two thesis summaries. Grade these summaries with the help of the 'Rubrics for evaluating the proposal qualities' (see Appendix G, Section 2), with special attention to embedding in the discipline and theory.

The double value of the proposal's literature review

A special point of attention is the multiple value of a literature review. If enough time is taken for this, this not only creates an important building block for the proposal. With a good literature review, an important text is written for the future thesis or its components, if you start drafting a thesis based on articles. This is a draft. Over the coming years, colleagues will publish articles and books that you will incorporate into an updated version of the literature review.

Your supervisor's quality expectations

In Appendix L, you will find the criteria used in the assessment of a literature review, the report of your literature search and the critical appraisals of the literature found. There is a good chance that your supervisor will not deviate much from this in the assessment of your work!

7.6 Originality

Future supervisors, admission committees or committees that award subsidies will assess your thesis plans on several qualities. In their journal article, 'What is originality in the humanities and the social sciences?' Guetzkow et al. (2004) show what the dominant assessment criteria are in the committees that must assess research proposals. Their research focused on the humanities and social sciences. However, the results of this research also apply to other disciplines. In their research, six criteria turned out to be dominant in the quality assessment of a research proposal: clarity, 'quality' (in all its different operationalizations), originality, significance, methods and feasibility.

In one part of your proposal, you will pay attention to the originality of the thesis plan. This criterion is often something that causes fear. By intuition you feel that the evaluators of your proposal will judge your plans on this criterion. You might blow this criterion up to mythological proportions and have no idea how to give it hands and feet.

Twenty-eight ways to be original

The research of Guetzkow et al. (2004) can bring a lot of peace to your fears. They show that in the assessors' practice many definitions of originality arise. In an overview they show 28 different types of originality. They distinguish seven main types of originality that can be operationalized further: an original approach, an understudied area, an original topic, an original theory, an original method, original data and original results (ibid.: 197).

You can specify these main types of originality by asking yourself questions such as: will I formulate new questions? Will I study aspects of my topic that have been understudied until now? Will I bring together theoretical insights in an unexpected way? Or will I use methods in an unexpected way? Most likely your topic is already original just because you will be collecting new data and providing new insights.

For more details on these 28 ways to be original, consult their article which is available as an open-source document on the internet: (https://www.researchgate.net/publication/241644109_What_Is_Originality_in_the_Social_Sciences_and_the_Humanities).

In this context, it may also be useful to address the issue of the relevance of the proposed research: the consequences in terms of understanding a phenomenon or its societal consequences, and its impact on our academic world and the broader world around us.

It is best to discuss originality and relevance with your peers, the Lab convener and supervisor after your first steps regarding the literature search and literature review and before submitting the proposal halfway.

7.7 From topic to question

After some time, you will have oriented yourself in the direction of specific research topics. Now the moment has come that you will learn how to formulate a research question about a topic or how to evaluate research questions that have been formulated by others, for example, your supervisors. Below, several types of research questions will be dealt with. Your main action will be to formulate diverse types of research questions on your research topic.

The following will lead you to that part of the proposal in which you formulate the core questions of your research and make clear which requirements the formulation of your questions must meet:

- Which central question would you like to answer with the research?
- How do you unfold the central question into sub-questions, so that the joint answers will generate the answer to the central question?

Preparatory reading

Booth et al. (2016: Chapter 3), 'From topics to questions'.
Chapter 4, Session 6 (From topic to questions).

Question Practicum

This is a brain exercise for questioning the subject of preference in diverse ways. Join The Question Practicum (Appendix K). You have reached the moment it will be possible to transform your major interest in a topic into several question options. Try to write down your interest (or aspects of it) in the format of each of the seven question options:

> For example: if my research preference would be a descriptive one, my leading research question could read as follows [..........], and my sub-questions as follows [1..........2..........3......].

Do not panic if an option doesn't link up with your interest or the intrinsic qualities of the topic. If a type really does not fit your research objective, leave it out.

If you hesitate regarding several possible research topics, just choose one to do this exercise in these Question Gymnastics. Send the result of your work to peers, your Lab convener and supervisors.

The aim of this exercise is to let you 'play' with different question type options. At the end, you will have to decide which question type and research perspective you feel most comfortable with and is most appropriate in view of your research goal. One tip: do not think in mutually exclusive question options. For example, whatever your ultimate research objective might be, descriptive questions will always figure somewhere in your overview of main question and sub-questions.

Types of questions

Which types of question can we distinguish? Meltzoff and Oost distinguish the following types of questions (Meltzoff, 2007: Chapter 2; Oost, 2003):

- *Existence questions*: 'Does x exist?' Important when existence or non-existence of something is controversial (Meltzoff, 2007).
- *Questions of description, classification and composition*: 'Is it variable or invariant? … What are the components that make up x?' (ibid.). 'What are its qualities, what characteristics does it have? How is it? What is it made of? Who or what does it involve? What does it look like?' (Oost, 2003).
- *Descriptive-comparative questions*: 'What are the differences? What are the similarities? In what ways are they different? In what ways do they overlap, are they the same?' (ibid.).
- *Relationship questions*: 'Is there a relationship between x and y?' (Meltzoff, 2007).
- *Causality questions*: 'Why is it so? How did it happen? What is this a consequence of? What reasons are there? What is its background? How could this happen?' (Oost, 2003).
- *Questions of evaluation*: 'What is its worth? How well does it work? … What are its advantages and disadvantages?' (Meltzoff, 2007).

Evaluating the quality of questions

A good starting point for evaluating the quality of the research questions is the work of Bryman (2008). According to Bryman, the research questions for a thesis or project should be clear, researchable, connected with theory and earlier research, linked with each other, have a potential for contributing to knowledge and find a balance between too narrow and too broad. In Appendix G, Section 3, you will find the criteria for evaluating your questions.

A special note on the relationship between the main question and the sub-questions. We always try to formulate an overarching question that we can only answer by answering several sub-questions. Do view it as a pyramid. At the top is the central research question. Below that, we formulate the sub-questions that we need to answer the main question. Often there is another layer of sub-questions underneath. We are strict about including the sub-questions. We can be in love with a sub-question and the material that we can collect for it, but if we do not need all of this to answer the main question ... cross it out! This keeps our project lean. Booth et al. (2016) also offer useful advice regarding what to avoid: questions whose answers are settled fact you could just look up; that can be answered too easily; questions that will not be answerable because we cannot find the data to answer the question; questions that are based on preference or taste, questions that make you read too many sources, questions for which you cannot get the sources your readers think are crucial, questions whose answer you cannot plausibly disprove.

> **Action**
>
> Write out the research question and the sub-questions for your research proposal, departing from a clear research problem and indicating the innovative character/relevance of your research and the way it is embedded in theory and existing literature (the literature overview is taken as a benchmark). You will start from the knowledge acquired in this section and Section 7.4 'Disciplinary embedding and the literature review'.

7.8 Something to fear: the theory

You have arrived at a part of the proposal that frightens many of you: THE THEORY. One of the explanations for this is the wide variety of views on what a theory is. I will go deeper into the definition of a theory as *a collection of well-motivated, disciplinary embedded and researchable propositions/theses that try to explain or try to understand a phenomenon*. My suspicion is that most of the PhD research is focused on collecting and analysing primary and secondary data for which propositions and working hypotheses are especially useful.

This section is related to Section 3 of the proposal: Description of the field of study, the existing body of knowledge and theoretical perspectives'. This part of the proposal is directly inspired by what you have read in the literature, the interviews you held, the meetings you had with your (possible) supervisor, and what you wrote down in other assignments. In this section you analyse the state of the (research) art regarding your topic. Essentially, this section is laying the foundation for your questions, your interest. The foundation for all this information is lying in your literature search, literature notes, critical appraisal and literature review.

In this section you will explain from which perspective you will try to answer your research questions, for example, explaining the theoretical foundations for a hypothesis, a research argument or a claim (Booth et al., 2016).

Different perspectives on theory

Pawson and Tilley (2008) make the lives of PhD candidates easier by making it clear that there are many different perspectives regarding the definition and role of the theory. For example, they distinguish the following meanings of theory:

- General orientations
- Ad hoc or ex post factum interpretations
- Empirical generalizations
- Axiomatic systems
- Hypotheses
- Explanations
- Paradigms
- Conceptual frameworks
- Causal propositions

You will discuss your own definition with your supervisor who will explain which traditions are leading in your own field of study and department. It is important and reassuring to know that there is not one sacred definition of theory. The crucial point is again that you do not assume that you already know what a theory is and what role it plays in your research. You will realize that your literature review is essential in developing your own theoretical ideas. Studying the research of others will give you a grip on the role of theory in research. Those researchers may also provide you with theoretical insights that are of direct use for your own future research.

Theory within a PhD research proposal: the propositions

In my own programme, I have always worked with the following working definition of the theory:

> A theory is a collection of well-motivated, disciplinary embedded and researchable propositions/theses that try to explain or try to understand, for example, the existence or non-existence of a problem, the similarities, and differences between A & B, the (in)effectiveness of a measure, the plausibility of a development, etc.

It is not my intention to focus on a specific interpretation of the term 'theory'. That is up to you and your research environment. It will help you to address the difference between theory and hypothesis in this regard as well as the role of theory in research. Bordens and Abbott (2008) distinguish between understanding, prediction, organizing and interpreting research results and generating research ('providing ideas for new research'). They conclude with the distinction between theory-driven versus data-driven research. This distinction comes close to the concept of 'grounded theory' that Glaser and Strauss launched in 1967 (revised in 2009): the discovery of theory from data systematically obtained from ... research. This approach can be especially useful in view of subjects where theories are not yet available for developing propositions, where neither the 'grand theories' nor 'theories of the middle range' can assist in formulating specific claims regarding our subject that has not been researched previously.

> **Action**
>
> Read literature on the role of theory in the scientific research in your discipline. These texts can be ones that deal with the role of the theory in a general sense, or in a specific domain, or in view of a specific topic.

Meeting colleagues: their view on theory

If you participate in the Proposal Lab, senior researchers or fellow PhD candidates will illustrate the role of the theory in their own research.

> **Action**
>
> If you work individually on your proposal in co-operation with a supervisor, it is attractive to attend meetings where colleagues present their research. Every university department organizes such meetings from time to time. With all these presentations, pay attention to the role of theory in the research presented, the type of theory and which role the theory is playing in terms of:
>
> - understanding;
> - prediction;
> - organizing and interpreting research results.

An opportunity for specifications: propositions, work hypotheses and claims

In Section 5 of the proposal, you will move to the formulation of your argument, central proposition, claim, etc. Many authors have given definitions of work hypotheses and claims.

We can think of the definition as given, for example, in the *Oxford Dictionary of Psychology* (Colman, 2009) where a hypothesis is defined as a tentative explanation for a phenomenon, subject to criticism by rational argument and refutation by empirical evidence.

A must-read for all of you is *The Craft of Research* by Booth et al. (2016). We already met them in Section 7.7 ('From topic to questions'). Here I focus on Part III of their book, 'Making an Argument': 'At the core of every research argument is the answer to your research question – your main claim.' Booth et al. explain how to evaluate the clarity and significance of the claim that answers your research question and that serves as the main point of your dissertation. They advocate a tentative answer to your research question to focus your research on the data that will assess and support its answer.

7.9 How to answer the questions: the material collection, the research design

At this moment you have reached a next stage in the development of your Research Proposal. You have found and studied the literature, you know why your research project is relevant, you are determined in your topic choice. Moreover, you have contacted experts, talked with peers and they all support your research ambitions. On top of this, you have found a good supervisor who is enthusiastic about your plans and your qualities.

You are approaching the real start of your project. There are some hurdles you must overcome before you can report about your plans in the format of a Research Proposal.

- You think, 'Yes, I have the questions, but which data do I need to answer my questions?'
- You are working under limits of time and feasibility, so you must limit yourself. You cannot study the whole world, all the cases, total history, you can't interview all the possible informants … you must work on a selection of units (countries, cases, persons, documents, periods, experiments), in other words: the sample.
- You think, 'Okay, I might have specified the data and the sample, but how then to collect my information, which methods of data collection and data analysis will I be using?'

Why is it important to offer our readers this information? We must comply with the important criteria in establishing and assessing the quality of our research. That starts with offering transparency on sampling and methods before we start the research (so that others can judge the quality of our approach and feasibility – ex ante evaluation) and after we have completed the project (so that others, for example, our supervisors, can evaluate the quality of our findings and report – ex post evaluation). Let us make this more specific, by referring to Bryman and what he tells us about the most prominent criteria for the evaluation of research: reliability, replication, and validity (2008: 31):

> *Reliability.* Reliability is concerned with the question of whether the results of a study are repeatable.

Validity. a) Measurement validity. b) Internal validity ... Does the conclusion regarding a causal relationship between variables holds water? c) External validity. Can the results of a study be generalized beyond the specific research context?

Your primary interlocutors

Even if you participate in a Proposal Lab, the senior and junior colleagues from your department will play the leading role here with a primary role for your supervisors. They will give feedback, discuss with you whether you are mastering the required research skills and give literature tips.

You may already have research experience and have had introductions to the distinctive design possibilities, methods and techniques in your discipline. Now you will apply any existing knowledge in your own research design.

> **Action**
>
> Contacts with your supervisors and peers offer you the opportunity to determine whether your knowledge in the aforementioned areas is indeed present and where additional training is necessary.

Information sources

Regarding the literature, consider the following. It is beyond the scope of a Proposal Lab to discuss in detail the research design options in different disciplines. A literature search with the keyword 'research design in [...]' will provide you with numerous literature suggestions within seconds regarding the research design in any discipline.

In Chapter 4, Session 8, you will find more detailed information about the research design in the proposal. Verschuren and Doorewaard (2005: 111–14) published an important book on research design. I summarize their most important recommendations and observations. In each research project, the researcher selects methods to obtain the research findings. The researcher will be guided by prior knowledge or theories about the phenomena under study. The researcher's ideas might be intuitive or formulated as propositions or working hypotheses. In that way the research process starts with a conceptual model of the object of research. That determines the questions that are to be answered and which procedures will be used to find answers to these questions. The research design shows the researcher's plan for collecting and organizing data and which specifics rules and procedures will be followed. Many alternatives are available regarding the nature of the research cases, the number of cases, the primary basis for selecting cases (sampling), basic sources of data, the methods of gathering the data, etc. Every decision should be well motivated in the proposal the candidates are preparing.

After the primary research question has been defined, we will formulate a number of sub-questions whose answers allow us to answer the main question at the end of the research project. Sometimes we are inclined to formulate more questions than we need to answer the main question. This is a 'red flag' moment.

After we have formulated the sub-questions – and sometimes there is even a layer of sub-sub-questions – we will determine what kind of material we need to answer the questions and how we are going to collect this material. All these points must be clearly stated in our research proposal.

Bryman (2008: 381) mentions quality criteria in view of your design:

1 How defensible are the design and sample of cases?
2 Sample composition – how well is the eventual coverage described?
3 Contexts of data sources – how well are they portrayed?
4 How well has a diversity of perspective been explored?
5 How well have details of data been considered?

Quality criteria

My teaching team at the Tilburg Law School developed rubrics for the evaluation of PhD proposals. I present one of these rubrics to clarify the requirements in view of the data collection:

1 Function of the research (describing, comparing, defining, evaluating, explaining, designing).
2 Sample (segment of the population [universe of units or objects] that is selected for research, for example, locations, periods, objects, actors, etc.).
3 The properties or attributes of object(s) of research (to be compared, described, evaluated, etc.).
4 Data collection methods.

Rubric on Methods section

1= Lack of methods section: Methods section showing hardly any information on research function, sample, object properties and methods.
2= Methods section lacking relevant information on the research function, sample, object properties and methods. And/or level of analysis needs improvement.
3= Methods section adequately clarifying research function, sample, object properties and methods. Level of analysis is satisfactory but is lacking details in motivation.
4= Methods section effectively clarifying research function, sample, object properties and methods. Level of analysis and motivation is good.
5= Methods section effectively clarifying research function, sample, object properties and methods. Level of analysis and motivation is excellent.

Application of insights

> **Action**
>
> Think about how you are going to answer the central research question (and sub-questions) of your research project. In other words, what data you will need to answer these questions, and what will be your research methods. Write your replies on one A4 sheet, bring it to the session of the Proposal Lab meeting and discuss it with your supervisor.

> **Action**
>
> Analyse two proposals written by your predecessors, paying particular attention to the data and methods section in these proposals and evaluate them. It is always about the following issues.
>
> - Can we read the central questions and sub-questions in the proposal?
> - Can we find justifications of the research (news value, social relevance, theoretical relevance)?
> - Can we see how the research is engaged in existing knowledge?
> - Is the necessary information about sources available?
> - Is the necessary information about the methods of data collection available?

There are three questions that we will repeat again and again:

- Is information about those issues present in our proposal (presence)?
- Is the choice explained (how something was done)?
- Is the choice justified (why that choice has been made)?

> **Action**
>
> Organize a meeting with a colleague and explain to each other the following:
>
> - what the central research question in your intended research is;
> - what the sub-research questions are;
> - which (methodological) steps you will take to answer these questions.
>
> After these pairwise discussions, organize a meeting with your supervisors and – if applicable – your Proposal Lab convener.

8 Anticipating problems and concerns

8.1 Experiences of your predecessors: the Proposal Halfway SWOT analysis

To give you an idea of the situation after about 4 months of working on a proposal, I present the results of a SWOT analysis that my colleagues and I performed in response to the Proposals Halfway received. How far were our Lab participants on the way to their proposal? What were we worried about?

Such a SWOT analysis is an attractive means of assessing a proposal in all its aspects. We not only indicate the points for improvement but are also explicit in our appreciation. What did my colleagues and I see after about 4 months of hard work? For you, the results of this analysis can function as a checklist to determine how far you are on your way to a nice result.

Strengths

- Originality of some topics as such (while other students must find the empty niche in a popular field).
- Independence and willingness to work hard.
- The willingness to offer each other peer support.
- Not being afraid to tackle challenges and big questions.
- Recognizing the importance of a clear definition of concepts.

Weaknesses

- Planning and time management.
- Not clearly understanding the meaning of a hypothesis in a research project.
- Implicit assumptions about the existence of a problem to be studied.
- Unspecified information about the data needed to answer research questions.
- Weak interest in explanatory aspects of a project.

Opportunities

- Connecting practical questions with theory ('why and how' questions instead of 'how should …').
- Literature study is okay in most cases – next step: writing a nice literature review.
- Consulting peers and external experts.
- Seeing a Master's programme and a PhD project as an integrated project (a Master's thesis could become a potential chapter of the PhD thesis).

Threats

- Unwillingness to make choices.
- The project is too big (feasibility!), and no alternative scenario is available if original planning turns out to be undoable.
- Insufficient embedding of research questions in the existing body of literature (specifying what is known and unknown).
- Lack of communication with the supervisor.
- Not showing uncertainty or hiding problems.
- Procrastination (for example, not being able to stop reading).
- Not being in contact with (other) experts.

8.2 Advice by your colleagues, being a bit further on the road

Here is some advice from your colleagues, who are a bit further down the road to the PhD proposal. This is a shortened version of a letter of nine pages that I compiled from contributions by supervisors and many PhD candidates, present at the PhD Day 2009 of the Medical-Educational PhD Candidates Network (Sonneveld, 2009):

> Dear fellow (future) PhD candidate,
>
> You are considering starting a PhD somewhere or you may have just started. I hope I reach you before you decide to accept a PhD position somewhere. Below are many practical tips for a PhD candidate who just has started the PhD project or is preparing it … The most important thing is to talk to PhD candidates who have been supervised by your intended supervisor. Then you get an idea of how you will probably receive support and guidance … Your research stands or falls with good supervision, both in terms of content and collaboration between the two people … I would certainly make sure that the supervisor does not have too many PhD candidates so that good supervision is possible. Look before you apply and get started.
>
> Financial conditions
>
> Regarding the financing: is it already in place for the entire period of the future project? And if so, who is financing the project, what is covered by that financing and what is not, and are there any special conditions or interests to consider? … Sometimes it happens that a project is initiated by a research group, whereby they take care of financing the first two years, with the expectation that financing for the last two years will be arranged with a yet-to-be-arranged outside subsidy provider … What happens if it is not possible to complete the financing in time? This can mean that as a PhD candidate you will spend a lot of time in your first year writing for such a grant, time that you cannot spend on doing research.

Click, and clear expectations

Whoever is going to do the supervision, I advise you in the first instance to pay attention to the click: can you get on well with each other, as people and as researchers? Invest in getting to know yourself and each other: what motivates, what appeals? You can make good use of this later; you will know better what you need and/or how you can approach your supervisor ... And perhaps the most important piece of advice I have: make mutual expectations explicit.

From a practical point of view, it is useful to know whether your supervisor already has experience in supervising PhD candidates. If that is not the case, you will have to do and ask much more yourself than if someone has already had supervised 10 PhD candidates.

A knowledgeable supervisor

What should you pay attention to? That the supervisor is knowledgeable in the field. The supervision must also ensure that you are sufficiently in line with the state of affairs in the research and build on that. The subject of research is critically examined, so that it is not only relevant for your department but also for the world. The good supervisor therefore also tries to help you place the research in a broader context.

Your network

During supervision, it is important that as a PhD candidate you have a network of other researchers with whom to spar and exchange from time to time... As a starter it is not easy to find your way in the world of publications. A supervisor should show you the way to publication opportunities.

Schedule

Monitor the time if you have other tasks besides your PhD work, i.e., teaching tasks. Before you know it, a lot of time and attention will go to the side tasks (which you also want to do as well as possible) while doing your research already requires a lot of attention, focus and effort.

In addition to any plan set up by others, make your own plan for the coming year. That gives you an overview. That means you must also plan for yourself the periodic evaluation moments. They don't look nice but are much needed; for yourself but also for keeping mutual expectations clear. Failure to evaluate periodically is not a sign of expertise or a high degree of independence!

The meetings

One of the most important things for managing a supervisor is that you have sufficient contact with each other. There must be an accessible contact to ask questions, especially in the first year. Is it someone who is very busy and who does not have time to consult with you? Then you must make clear agreements about this. Plan once every two weeks a fixed appointment to discuss things. It is good to make an agenda for all conversations, so that you can clearly steer the conversation in a direction, and you get everything you want out of it. Send it in advance, so everyone knows where they stand. In view of important conversations (e.g., when you and all supervisors are together), it is useful to write a report of the conversation and send it to everyone for approval.

The supervision style

One supervisor thinks that you should first try to figure things out yourself, the other thinks that muddling is a waste of time. You can learn a lot from both, but in a different way. Just try everything in the first place, then you will notice what works. The supervisors here often find it better if you come up with a concrete suggestion, then they have something to shoot on. They prefer not to have a question along the lines of 'should it be this way, or that way, ...?'.

Work pressure and teaching

Work pressure is an aspect of a PhD project that should not be underestimated. Make agreements: what does/doesn't belong to your research, which side tasks you can/don't perform, how much time do you spend on such matters? Find the balance between watching time and learning as much as possible ... As a PhD candidate employed by a university, you are often also expected to teach. Sometimes it has already been contractually stipulated how many hours that may be but ask future fellow PhD candidates from the same research group whether the practice also corresponds to what is on paper.

Issues

A supervisor who meets all the wishes and requirements as I have described them above is truly a 'dream supervisor'. There are certainly a few of these around, but issues may arise over the course of 4 years that create a dark cloud over your partnership. I would like to conclude here with three situations that often occur between PhD candidates and supervisors. On a case-by-case basis, I'll indicate what you can do best. In all of this, realize that problems seem to happen to all of us. Remember that they can be a 'natural' part of growing up in a subject, doing complex research, and belong to the different phases in a PhD candidate's own development.

Case 1. Expertise

You slowly but surely come to know much more about the subject than your supervisors. You get the feeling that there is a lack of good substantive feedback. How bad is that? What to do?

- Look for expansion of your network and discuss it with your (co)supervisors. They can introduce you to other experts or relevant institutions.
- It seems essential to me that you continuously maintain communication. In case they can't or do not want to make time for this, keep informing them about substantive steps you are taking, relevant publications that are already there and the substantiation of your own new insights.

- If it becomes problematic and unworkable, involve others. As support or as an independent third party ... In many graduate schools these kinds of specialists do exist.
- If the situation really becomes untenable, then ending this working relationship is ultimately the adequate solution (for all parties). This also requires care and integrity.

Case 2. Conflicting advice, lack of communication in your team

In our hectic academic world, this may be a more common problem than the first. You just don't manage to get your three companions around the table at the same time. You notice that the supervisors hardly talk to each other about your work. All of this leads to repeatedly receiving conflicting advice. Even worse if you feel like your supervisors haven't read your work when you get together. What to do?

- Do not become a ping-pong ball.
- Clearly state the problem, also indicate why it is a problem for you.
- Ask your co-supervisor/daily supervisor to intervene.
- If the problem arises at a later stage in your project: ultimately make the research decisions yourself and email them to your supervisors with an argumentation. Finish (politely!) with a sentence that shows that if one of your supervisors wants something different, they will really have to discuss this with you.
- Finish the co-operation if there is absolutely no other way.
- Avoid this problem by doing the following:
  - Determine at the beginning who does what and decides (division of roles).
  - Indicate clearly (but politely) at the start of your project that anyone who wants influence must also participate in meetings.
  - Plan the appointments well in advance from the start ... if your supervisors cannot get together at all, then there is something else going on than too-full agendas.
  - Record agreements in an email, and make sure that everyone will give their storable consent.

Case 3. The bigger picture

Your supervisors are constantly focused in their supervision and comments on parts of the dissertation, the chapters are often published first as articles. You doubt whether they have enough eye for the dissertation as a whole. You start to worry about this because you realize that the Doctorate Committee will express an opinion about your final product from an 'overall view'. What is the best thing to do in this situation?

- Think in advance of the red line that runs between your articles. After all, those are the chapters of your dissertation.
- It is not only the task of the supervisors to keep an eye on the line; the PhD candidate must also do this him or herself.
- Your research questions are leading and overarching. So, keep an eye on them.

Finally, I can say to you: ask! I think most supervisors are of good will, but like you and me, they can't read minds. So, ask specifically for what you need. There is a good chance that you will get it … It is important that you also dare to say 'no' to some things, or that you ask further questions if things are unclear.

Just ask nicely :).

If you want to make (and keep) your supervisor happy, do just a little more than was agreed in the previous meeting.

Best regards and good luck!

Your future colleague.

8.3 Which travel guides to read?

In the preceding sections I mentioned several authors who have written important books on preparing and conducting a PhD project. I mention them and some others here again:

Aveyard, H. (2007) *Doing a Literature Review in Health and Social Care: A Practical Guide*. Maidenhead: Open University Press.
Becker, H.S. (1998) *Tricks of the Trade: How to Think About Your Research While You're Doing It*. Chicago: The University of Chicago Press.
Booth, W.C., Colomb. G.G., Williams. J.M., Bizup, J. and FitzGerald, W.T. (2016) *The Craft of Research* (4th edn). Chicago: University of Chicago Press.
Brewer, R. (2007) *Your PhD Thesis: How to Plan, Draft, Revise and Edit Your Thesis*. Abergele: Studymates Limited.
Delamont, S., Atkinson, P. and Parry, O. (2004) *Supervising the Doctorate: A Guide to Success*. London: The Society for Research into Higher Education.
Gosling, P. and Noordam, B. (2006) *Mastering Your PhD: Survival and Success in the Doctoral Years and Beyond*. Berlin: Springer-Verlag.
Greenhalgh, T. (2010) *How to Read a Paper: The Basics of Evidence-Based Medicine* (4th edn). Oxford: Wiley-Blackwell.
Lovitts, B.E. (2007) *Making the Implicit Explicit: Creating Performance Expectations for the Thesis*. Sterling, VA: Stylus Publishing.
Phillips, E.M. and Johnson, C.G. (2022) *How to Get a PhD: A Handbook for Students and Their Supervisors* (7th edn). Maidenhead: Open University Press.
Punch, K.F. (2016) *Developing Effective Research Proposals* (3rd edn). London: Sage.
Verschuren, P. and Doorewaard, H. (2005) *Designing a Research Project*. Utrecht: Lemma.

Watts, M. (2001) The Holy Grail: In pursuit of the dissertation proposal. University of California. Available at: https://dusk.geo.orst.edu/prosem/PDFs/InPursuitofPhD.pdf. (accessed 22 August 2021).

8.4 Anxieties are normal

In Chapter 4, Section 2, 'The first individual feedback meeting', I will give an overview of the most important uncertainties and questions that you can struggle with as a starting proposal author. I outline the essentials here to show you that you are not alone:

- Now and again, the questions may arise among you whether a certain type of research or specific topic would be acceptable. You may assume certain research preferences on the part of the supervisors.
- Many of you mention finding a well-defined subject and key question as one of your main problems.

Most of you will recognize some weaker qualities in your self-evaluation:

- Weak management qualities: weak time management, difficulty in dealing with deadlines and the psychological background of these weaknesses (perfectionism as a theme!).
- Difficulties in bringing order to your thoughts: how to put ideas on paper, difficulties arriving at a logical text.
- Difficulties with focus, topic, main question: bringing too many things together, losing the plot in writing, a proposal being too broad, difficulties in narrowing down.
- Expressions of perfectionism: not wanting to stop, there is always something to improve, 'Setting my bars very high, frustration in case of non-achievement of goals' or 'Unfinished work drives me crazy'.
- Doubts about having control over the matter of study: problems with managing amounts of literature, 'Drowning myself in books'.
- Existential doubts about research qualities: 'Do I possess the intellectual capacities to become a researcher?'

Know that in most cases, everything turned out nicely at the end of the proposal journey! Know that the supervisors will be happy to provide you with all possible support when it comes to substantive issues. However, if personal psychological problems are involved, they become reluctant. They are not practising psychologists.

8.5 Getting a grip on the essentials of a successful journey: Becker's Machine Trick

In our teaching, we asked our respondents to explain their positive and critical evaluations of their supervisors and their own efforts in developing a PhD proposal or PhD project. Reporting all their praise and criticisms would lead to an endless list of dos and don'ts. Instead, we will do the Machine Trick. This has been suggested by one of the most original thinkers in sociology: Howard Becker (1998: 39). To get a full grip on what matters in, for example, a successful supervision and completion of a PhD project, we don't ask ourselves what the best strategies and conditions would be. To get a sharp focus on what really matters, we ask ourselves how a machine should look if we want to make a supervision and our working on our PhD proposal fail. Imagining such a machine gives us a good reason for including what we otherwise would leave out while thinking about improvements. Of course, Howard Becker tells us, we don't really want these results but engage in this machine-designing exercise as a way of systematically looking for everything that contributes to the occurrence of, in this case, the success or failure of a PhD project or, in this case, the development of a PhD proposal.

We ask ourselves the following question. How should the supervision machine and our proposal machine look in order to make our proposal project a failure? Here are the components of that machine:

1 The supervisor accepts you as a (potential) doctoral candidate, knowing as little as possible about your ideas about the topic.
2 Your admission or acceptance as a candidate is only based on written material – you don't see each other during a face-to-face interview!
3 In case of foreign candidates – your proficiency in English is not tested.
4 Being supervised by one single supervisor who has another nine PhD candidates and is not sharing supervision with colleagues.
5 You and your supervisor don't care about the planning of your PhD project,
6 ... and will see each other every two or three months (maximum!).
7 You will find out completely by yourself which proposal criteria will be used when progress is monitored.
8 Of course, you and the supervisor don't check before the start if you possess the basic qualities for designing a research project,
9 ... and you accept gladly the supervisor's poisoned chocolate by letting you read and read and read as long as possible (no exercises in writing!).
10 Your supervisor furthers your focus and concentration by hindering as much as possible communication with other specialists or peers about your proposal or dissertation in progress. Isolation always works marvellously!
11 And, please, commit yourself to other heavy study obligations that hinder your time investment in the proposal.
12 Success will be guaranteed even more if the supervisor lets you swim and suffer in case of a failing proposal development. The supervisor doesn't intervene but lets you struggle in despair.
13 And, please, supervisor, don't show trust in your candidate, even if things are going very well.

Are there other components you can think of?

9 What we will know at the end of the proposal journey

And then the proposal journey is over. What do we know, then, about the attractiveness of our subject, about our own strengths and weaknesses, and about the viability of the working relationship with our supervisor?

9.1 Will a PhD project suit us?

At the end of this proposal journey, we also know whether we want to work on the same project for about 4 years. I sometimes compare PhD research with a 10,000-metre speed skating race. Some of you find this appealing, others prefer driving 1,500 metres, shorter research projects. One does not necessarily exclude the other. In a dissertation culture that is increasingly based on writing articles, it is quite possible to divide a project into several parts. As a result, you will round off interim results. That is a significant difference in comparison with those who start writing a monographic dissertation and must wait about four years before they feel like it is finished.

Anyway, at the end of the Proposal Journey we will know much better if we want to work on a research project for 4 years or longer (part-time).

9.2 Checking progress

In Chapter 4, Section 2, 'The first individual feedback meeting', I report on student evaluations of their own research qualities. If certain topics are familiar to you, it is interesting to chart your progress on these components after the Proposal Lab or the completion of an individual proposal process. Probably you will feel much comfortable now. At the start, the students mentioned the following as concerns:

- misunderstandings as regards whether a certain type of research or specific topic would be acceptable;
- finding a well-defined subject and key question (mentioned as their main problem);
- familiarity with a subject;
- weak management qualities;
- difficulties in bringing order to thoughts;
- difficulties with focus, topic, main question;
- expressions of perfectionism;
- doubts about having control over the matter of study;
- worries about qualities of judgement;
- existential doubts about research qualities.

How do you feel about these points at the end of the proposal journey?

9.3 Having a proposal, but no opportunity to implement it

When we start working on a PhD proposal, we are rarely 100 per cent sure whether we can implement this project. The proposal can be the material that you hand over when applying for a PhD position or at the start of the research stage of a PhD trajectory that has already commenced. Or you and your supervisor will apply for an external grant for this research. In these cases, the outcome is uncertain. But know that your efforts have never been in vain. An exceptionally talented participant in one of my Proposal Labs concluded with a good proposal for which no funding turned out to be available. Then her supervisor alerted her to another project. For this, too, she had to formulate her research plans in detail. Her previous proposal experiences enabled her to respond to this assignment in a very efficient manner, and within a couple of months; thus admission to the new project became a fact.

9.4 What are my strengths and weaknesses?

At the end of this proposal journey, you will have a good idea of your own strengths and areas for improvement. You can use the SWOT analysis, Appendix P, to run through the points that matter most in relation to the future PhD project.

Implicitly or explicitly, the points for attention in this SWOT analysis will also be the points that you and the supervisors look at when deciding whether to continue the collaboration.

9.5 What is my supervisor's perspective?

Consult Chapter 5 where you can read how supervisors distinguish types of PhD candidates from each other and which predictors of success and problems they see. In their words: are you a certain winner, a topic hopper, a promising but fragile talent, or a talented disappointer?

4 The Proposal Lab sessions and feedback meetings

> **Reading tip**
>
> This chapter is written from the perspective of the Proposal Lab convener. In terms of content, it is also of direct importance for the participants in the Lab, individual students, and PhD candidates who are preparing a PhD proposal, and their supervisors.

1 Session 1: in search of our research topic

You have probably already spoken with the participants in this programme during the admission procedure. If the admission is the result of a written procedure, you will see this candidate for the first time today. The participants themselves probably don't know each other yet, with a few exceptions. This first meeting is therefore a real introduction to the convener(s), the fellow participants, and the programme.

1.1 Script for the first meeting
1. Welcome. The teacher introduces himself or herself.
2. The participants interview each other. 'Try to collect answers from six colleagues you don't know yet, on the following questions:
   - Why did you choose this programme?
   - Do you already have experience with doing research?
   - Do you already have an idea about a subject for future research?
   - What role does this programme play in your future plans?
   - Do you want to get a PhD?
   - What do you think is the most difficult when doing research?
3. Inventory round. Per participant: which answers provided you with inspiring insights?

4. What do we already know about doing research? Compose four subgroups:
   - Groups A and B: Ask the participants to formulate what they think are the key elements of a scientific investigation in their discipline in a rough topic exploration matrix. The aim is to let them look back on previous research experiences and have them translate these into the steps that must be followed in their own new research. It will turn out that the group already has a good sense of the core elements of research in their discipline. The purpose of this inventory is to activate this knowledge.
   - Group C: Ask these participants what can go wrong when doing an investigation in their discipline.
   - Group D. The Machine Trick. See Chapter 3, Section 8.5. The aim is to find out what can best be done to make an investigation fail (Becker 1998: 39).

The groups write their findings on large Post-its. Then we cluster their findings. The interesting question is whether the findings revolve around the main elements of our programme.

5. Break for lunch. The convener arranges the incoming Post-its.
6. The core elements of the programme. Introduction by the teacher. As a stepping-stone, the teacher comments on the main findings of the four issues when doing research and the building blocks of the Proposal Lab.
7. Introduction by the teacher: On the way to a topic choice and proposal, see paragraph 1.2. The teacher presents the topic exploration and development of a research proposal as a quasi-research exercise as such. During this introduction, the teacher hands out a 'best practice' PhD proposal by one of their predecessors, to be skimmed by the participants. This is to give them a picture of what you expect them to have produced around 6–8 months later.
8. In pairs, the participants individually complete the Rough Topic Exploration Matrix (see paragraph 4).
9. In conclusion, you prepare your participants for the individual meetings you will have with them in 2 weeks. They will have completed or updated the Snapshot and the Rough Topic Exploration Matrix by then. In that individual session, you will discuss these documents with them. You offer them also some study recommendations regarding the timing of efforts in the coming months, the timely start with the searching and studying of the literature, and the exploration of who might act as their future supervisor.

1.2 Lecture suggestion: the development of a proposal as exploratory research

Reassurance

In Session 1 of our programme, we show the contours of the interim product that must be submitted after a few months (the Proposal Halfway) and the product, the PhD proposal. These products do not differ in terms of issues to be dealt with. We do not slowly but surely inform our students about what we expect at the end of the program. No, from day one we make clear to them what the product should look like and how all parts of the programme prepare them for a well-justified research plan.

> **Action**
>
> Preferably you present them with a proposal form. You can find an example in Appendix I. This document not only presents the outline of a proposal. We also present the rubrics on which a proposal is assessed.
>
> You will see that these proposal components and the quality criteria correspond to what is customary in the world of grant applications for research. You adjust the information to the specific requirements in your own situation. This session, you offer your participants a helicopter view on the proposal components. In the Session, you will go into the details.
>
> Reassure your participants. They will feel overwhelmed by the information at this first meeting. Early September, I always tell them:. 'At the end of October, you will feel a sense of panic ... you will wonder how the hell this should end ... but you must know that you will proudly hand in a first version a proposal in April of the following year.'
>
> To illustrate this, in this first session, you hand out an example, a good proposal made by someone else in an earlier programme. This illustrates how their predecessors have fared well.
>
> In the continuation of this first session, we will present our travel guide. We go from station to station, accept nothing as already known or as a matter of course: the journey to a proposal.

Sudden genius doesn't exist

In 'Sudden Genius?' Andrew Robinson (2010) describes 'the gradual path to creative breakthroughs'. He analyses ten breakthroughs in the arts and sciences, from Leonardo da Vinci, via Marie Curie to Henri Cartier-Bresson. His study leads to the conclusion:

> Among all the patterns observable in exceptional creativity, perhaps the most intriguing is the so-called ten-year rule of breakthroughs ... it states that a person must persevere with learning and practising a craft or discipline for about ten years before he or she can make a breakthrough.
>
> (ibid.: xxxiii)

By analogy, the chance that you will encounter a 'sudden genius' among your prospective PhD candidates, someone who contacts you with a fantastic PhD plan, is negligible. You may recognize a 'born talent' and at the end of your programme you will be able to distinguish 'certain winners'. But none of your participants can come up with a good thesis plan on their own. None of them will know what is expected from him or her based on intuition. And you cannot assume that your participants just know how a literature review should be composed or what a research plan should look like. This is even more true for participants who have not studied at your faculty and who do not have, through careful attention and intuition, some idea of the local requirements set for a research plan. To rationalize the journey to a research plan, I have therefore presented the search for a research topic and plan as exploratory study. A good idea and a good plan do not come to us spontaneously but are created by a systematic approach. It all starts with a topic. Three starting positions are conceivable: (1) your participant already has a clear-cut idea about a subject; (2) the participant finds ten different topics interesting; or (3) the participant is still completely in the dark.

Types of topic exploration and the research file

The exploration of possible topics varies, depending on this starting situation. In the first place, I distinguish an exploration that can lead to a confirmation of the subject we are so enthusiastic about. We investigate the feasibility, the attractiveness (for example, has it been done before?), whether it can be guided and supported by a supervisor, and whether it connects with a research programme in the faculty or research group. As a thought experiment, we also deliberately look for reasons why this is not a good topic. Thus, we avoid the pitfall of not looking for creative disagreement.

In addition, there is the pure exploration. We have no idea about a subject yet. How do we define such an exploration? Based on Stebbins (2001: 3), in this Proposal Lab I would define the exploration of possible research topics as a research exercise as such. The essentials of a research design apply:

- What is the main *question you want to answer by the exploration?*
- How are your interests *embedded*?
    - in your study biography
    - in your social interests and activities
    - in the literature
    - in the intellectual environment.
- *Are you able to explain the relevance of the topic exploration* for you and possible supervisors, in other words, can you explain your motivation?
- *What information* do you need to decide on the topic?
- *Which methods* will you use to collect that information?
- *How will you report* on a well-reasoned topic choice?

Which exploration techniques do you suggest to your students? It is wise to keep a 'research file'. Wright Mills (1970) described this in his chapter, 'On intellectual craftmanship'. He suggests writing down anything that comes to mind about a potential topic in a research file and fill it with random ideas about subjects, newspaper or magazine clippings, notes from scholarly books and articles and snippets of conversations with people. If your participants are still considering different topics, let them keep different research files and write down their enthusiasm for a subject. If they keep such a diary for a few months and write down random ideas about the subjects, they will probably see what fascinates them time and time again and might possibly become a subject for their proposal. Through a regular re-reading of the notes, literature annotations and interview reports, they will discover lines and patterns, leading to a well-reasoned choice of subject.

Regarding the sources that we are going to consult, we have several options (Booth et al., 2016):

- finding what interests other researchers;
- skimming journals;
- asking questions suggested by sources (see, for example, the concluding discussion paragraph in many journal articles);
- talking with practitioners;
- browsing through textbooks and handbooks;
- attending lectures;
- asking colleagues about the most contested issues in the field;
- finding a relevant internet discussion list, browsing its archives, looking for matters of controversy or uncertainty;
- surfing the websites of departments at major universities.

Searching their interests, they can be led by a set of questions:

- What topics do you already know something about?
- What would you like to know more about? A place? A person? A time? An object? An idea? A process?
- Are you aware of a discussion about the issues that interest you?
- What issues have you debated with others, then found that you couldn't back up your views?
- What issues do other people misunderstand?
- What topic is your supervisor working on? Would the supervisor like you to explore a part of it?
- Does your library have rich resources in some field?

It may happen that your participants return to you not with one subject but with seven. How then to make the final choice? Howard Becker (1986: 54) made a great suggestion for this:

> Write whatever topic comes into your head, in no more than one or two sentences. Few of you will get past twenty or twenty-five ... before you will see that they share two or three central ideas, which are almost always variations on a common theme that interests you very much.

Make your participants practise this type of exercise in an analysis of their own earlier papers and reports to see if there are core elements in their interests.

Various obstacles can arise in this topic exploration: the topic is too broad ... we can't find literature on our topic – we must broaden the search field ... we can't find a supervisor ... our preferred topic has been done before ... We can also encounter problems in the personal sphere. Preparing a thesis plan asks for a change of study style. We must shift from a more consumptive study attitude to one where production and daring to rely on intuition and independence are central.

Managing the process

You also give your students some tips regarding the management of the process and their supervisor, as soon as it has become clear who would be the best candidate for the supervision. Here are some golden tips:

- Never show up without a suggestion from your side regarding topics you like to discuss with your supervisor or Lab convener.
- If you do produce something – pre-evaluate your work.
- Set an agenda for meetings with potential supervisors – make clear what you would like to discuss.
- Make an analysis of your meeting later: make notes and ask for comment.
- Make your planning obvious, distinguishing stages and products.
- Make your supervisor function better:
  - Agree on written comments on you work.
  - You make a report on the meeting.
  - The quality of feedback is crucial.

You will come back to this in Chapter 4, Session 2 (Planning in practice), on p. 97. You will also find much more information in Chapter 3 (Sections 5.2 and 5.3 on what supervisors and students expect from each other, on pp. 47–48).

For your students it will be a great relief to discover that you are fully aware of the complexities of this topic exploration phase. In the next part of Session 1, you will invite them to brainstorm about possible topics.

1.3 In-session activity: the first station, a rough topic exploration

In this programme, we do not assume that the participants have already chosen a topic for their research. In the first phase, we will support them in exploring their interests.

> **Action**
>
> During the first meeting they will complete the Rough Topic Exploration Matrix in pairs. This means that the participants are already exchanging ideas about finding a topic and laying the foundation for the individual conversation with the Lab convener that will follow shortly. In Appendix E, you will find this text in matrix format, to be distributed to the participants during this first session. The core issue in the Rough Topic Exploration is the search for sources of inspiration:
>
> - the student's social interests;
> - earlier products of study;
> - meetings with peers;
> - possible research environments;
> - a literature search 'light';
> - concrete cases or examples in the student's fields of interest.
>
> After this pairwise brainstorming, you invite your students to present one of their embryonic ideas: a topic they like to study, what they want to find out and how this might help others to understand the how and why of the issue.

1.4 Literature suggestions

For the participants, conveners and supervisors:

Booth et al. (2016)
Brewer (2007).

For conveners, supervisors (optional):

Wright Mills (1970)
Stebbins (2001)
Becker (1986; 1998).

2 The first individual feedback meeting: getting a feeling for your student's qualities and interests

2.1 Preparation and implementation

Immediately after the first meeting, the conveners have individual feedback discussions with all students. It is a clever idea to always have these conversations with student duos. Students also learn a lot about what teachers and fellow student discuss with each other. Moreover, the person who is not 'on the turn' takes notes for the colleague. This changes after 30 minutes.

This conversation focuses on two documents the students have sent to the teachers in advance:

- *The Snapshot* (a form that the student has completed before Session 1. In that document the student discusses their previous research activities, research interests, strengths, and weaknesses). See Appendix D.
- *The Rough Topic Exploration Matrix* (in the first meeting the student made notes about how they intend to approach the topic of the exploration). See Appendix E.

It is a nice idea to formulate the questions that the conveners should be able to answer after each interview:

1 Has the student already chosen a definitive subject?
2 Has the student decided on a specific disciplinary area within which a specific subject must be chosen?
3 Is the issue of the subject completely open?
4 Does the student have a clear picture of how to organize the topic exploration?
5 Does the student have a clear picture regarding people to consult? Is the student familiar with the library? (Check this especially in the case of newcomers, international students.)
6 Does the student already know which function to assign to the future proposal? (Stand-alone exercise, preparation for Master's thesis, PhD project or application elsewhere?)
7 Does the student also focus on possibilities other than just the possibilities that your department offers to conduct the research in the future (as, or instead of, a PhD project)? In other words: is the student betting on multiple horses?
8 Are there things that can hinder the writing of a good proposal?
9 Are there students within the programme who can benefit a lot from each other in the further development of their research ideas?

It can be useful to make notes regarding these points.

2.2 Results

Here you will find some of my observations. In retrospect, the triad of Snapshot/Rough Topic Exploration Matrix/First Individual Feedback Meeting is of great value to get a picture of the strengths and weaknesses of the students early in the programme (see Table 4.1).

Of course, there is also the one student who does not mention any weakness. We will see.

Table 4.1 Summary of students' strengths and weaknesses

Topic	Strengths and weaknesses
Diversity	Consider in the further organization of your programme the great diversity of subjects your group of students wants to study. In the coming sessions it will be impossible to focus on a limited set of subjects or methodological options. Sometimes, people know which area they want to work in. Sometimes, several areas are being considered. Some are already quite certain about the subject they want to tackle. Others hesitate about two or three topics. Some might prefer a qualitative style of research, others feel themselves more at ease in a quantitative or experimental research design.
Misunderstandings	Here and there, the questions may arise among students whether a certain type of research or specific topic would be acceptable. They may assume certain research preferences on the part of the supervisors. That might be happening if they contact potential supervisors, but as a Lab convener your agenda is open.
Peer support	Opportunities become visible for peer communications. For example, several students are interested in a similar subject. Students can also be important to each other because they have experiences in an area where a colleague wants to do research.
A major shared problem: starting the investigation	Many cite finding a well-defined subject and key question as one of their main problems.
Differences in familiarity with a subject	You will meet students who are already familiar with a topic, have practical experiences, have previously written about it (for example, in the context of an earlier thesis), and those who are in an initial stage of subject demarcation.
Your impressions after this first feedback meeting	Probably, you will formulate some 'working hypotheses' as to the qualities of your students: • There are candidates who inspire your trust because they are driven by a more demarcated subject and earlier study activities in the same area. • There are the candidates who convince you, but more on basis of their personal qualities than because of a grip on the subject or the trajectory that can lead to a choice. • There are candidates who make a weak impression. • There are candidates who are still question marks to you. Take care that these first impressions do not become a definitive judgement. Students in all categories can surprise you during your programme.

(Continued)

Table 4.1 (Continued)

Topic	Strengths and weaknesses
Weaker qualities that students might mention in their self-evaluation	1. Weak management qualities: • weak time management; • insufficient dealing with deadlines; • the psychological background of these weaknesses (perfectionism as a theme!). 2. Difficulties in bringing order to their thoughts: • difficulty putting ideas on paper; • difficulties achieving a logical text; • leaving limited time to write a paper. 3. Difficulties with focus, topic, main question: • difficulty in defining a narrow enough topic or choosing a manageable subject; • unable to narrow the research field; • not knowing how to start working on project; • not finding a relevant research question; • problem narrowing down the research question. 4. Perfectionism: • not wanting to stop, there is always something to improve; • 'setting my bars very high, frustration in case of non-achievement of goals'; • 'unfinished work drives me crazy'; • 'after finishing a paper, suddenly being not very satisfied, reviewing at the last minute, my paper becoming incoherent'; • 'being a perfectionist, hard for me to judge a task as finished and to progress to the next one. Wasting time.' • Over-exhaustiveness, for example, in a literature study. 5. Doubts about having control over the matter of study: • problems with managing the amount of literature; • having a lack of background knowledge; • no in-depth knowledge of a major topic yet; • difficulties in finding relevant sources. 6. Worries about qualities of judgement: • lacking skills of judging. 7. Existential doubts about research qualities: • do I possess the intellectual capacities to become a researcher?

2.3 Organizing the conversation

We distinguish two voices in the conversation. The student would like to know what we think about the subject or subjects. On our side, we want to form a picture of the student's plan of action to come to a topic.

There is a danger that the Lab conveners and supervisors will flood the student with suggestions if they feel that the student has no concrete ideas yet. They can be tempted to do so if the student has provided little information on paper, knows little to say in the conversation or is placing himself or herself in a passive position. The Lab conveners and supervisors can also end up in the strongly suggesting role if the student has very grand plans that call for specification.

In case of two conveners or supervisors being present, it is a good sign if they become enthusiastic, enter discussions with each other and produce countless suggestions. The student is on the way to an interesting topic. Yet in this case, we must remember that it is *the student* who soon will have to write a well-reasoned topic choice. It must remain *their* subject. The conversation can therefore get out of hand in two types of situations: (1) the teachers feel that they must save the student already from the very start; or (2) the teachers are so enthusiastic about the subject that they start overloading the student with all kinds of well-meant suggestions. This is the risk of taking over!

The interview can also have the function of helping the student prepare for a first interview with a possible supervisor. We can hold a mirror up to the student, saying: 'If you start the conversation in the same way as you do now, you will not get the best out of that conversation!'

The Rough Topic Exploration Matrix also shows whether students have an idea of who can function as a supervisor, aside from the Lab convener(s). The supervisors are the people who guide the student in the subject exploration and the writing of the final proposal.

The key point is that we must ensure that no 'orphans' walk around in our programme, students about whom nobody cares regarding the substance of their research interests.

2.4 The value of a typology

Would it be possible to design a typology of the students based on the Snapshot, the Rough Topic Exploration Matrix and the first Feedback interview? Could we already formulate indications as to what we can expect? The danger of this exercise is that we will act according to the first impressions and draw premature conclusions. However, these first impressions, working hypotheses as regards the student's qualities, can enable us to support the student in a more focused way.

Alarming combinations of indicators can be:

- The student has an idea as to the area in which the candidate wants to move, AND does not mention a specific subject and reports a lack of work discipline.
- The student has no concrete idea AND no concrete idea whom to approach AND is having difficulties in getting ideas down on paper.
- The student has no concrete idea AND doesn't know whom to approach AND is completely passive in communication.

- The student combines not having a topic idea AND a lack of work discipline.
- The student has no topic idea AND suffers from perfectionism.
- The student is panicking in uncertainty.

Even though we may be able to distinguish types of worry, there may also be one student's prototype for whom we may have grand expectations:

> Has already research experience + is reporting strength in structuring + has no time management problems + has at least an idea as to the area where one wants to be active (the subject can still come) + has a clear picture of the topic exploration approach + has an idea whom to contact.

2.5 Strong qualities of the students (self-reported)

In the Snapshot, the students also sketched a picture of the personal and intellectual qualities that they consider to be the strongest. They feel that these are the essentials of bringing a research project to a successful conclusion!

Working attitude

- Motivation.
- Discipline; working attitude; thorough and precise; iron discipline; accuracy.
- Time management.
- Stamina; hard working; determined.
- Work ethics, finishing papers as early as possible.
- Exactness, secure nature; perfectionist, always trying to improve the results one has reached.

Good interaction with other researchers

- Reacting well to feedback; open to other opinions; open to constructive comments/suggestions about their work, working attitude.
- Independent.
- Team worker.

Ability to structure and analyse

- Rapidly understanding core issue and inherent logic; differentiating key issues from side issues; analytical way of thinking; good analytical skills, ability to distinguish essentials from side issues.
- Structured and organized.
- Explains the matter in a clear and logical manner, reader can follow clear outline.

Distance and critical capacity

- Capable of preventing their view dominating sound information from others; can depict an objective picture of research object and findings.
- Critical way of looking at the subject.
- Loves the critical analysis of source material, the reading between the lines in texts.

Familiarity with research

- Research skills, research techniques, curiosity, knowledge of structuring scientific work; having conducted empirical research, interview skills; seeing and creating structure when doing research.
- Detailed and thorough in preliminary research.
- Heuristic research experience: using library and archival catalogues, bibliographies, literary databases.
- Having produced interesting conclusions; having said something new in the researched area.

Ability to control information

- Ability to search for a variety of sources.
- Capable of taking in a heavy load of information without the risk of drowning in it.
- Borrowing from different disciplines; finding sources, combining and using them; linking various sources of information.

Communicative qualities

- Language – clarity in writing and speech with respect to findings; ability to clearly formulate the ideas that one has in mind; writing skills; writing style that has been complimented.

2.6 Aftercare

It is conceivable that the teachers become worried during this meeting about the grip a student has on the trajectory that should lead to a topic choice a couple of months after the start of our programme. In some cases, it is wise to make a check with the student some time after this first feedback meeting. It is important not to assume that after this first meeting, they understand exactly what is expected from them. And do not be fooled by the desire to 'keep up appearances', pretending to know what is expected, on the student's part during that first meeting.

3 Session 2: meeting and interviewing researchers and planning the proposal

3.1 Pre-session assignment

Reading literature on structured interviewing (for example, Bryman, 2008).

Pre-session assignment: preparing interview questions for interviewing peer and draft of an email for interviewing experts and supervisors.

3.2 Script for Session 2

- *Part one (morning)*: researchers in action: Your colleagues [x] and [y] will introduce several types of research in your discipline. They will use examples of their own research or projects by close colleagues. We will see how the biographies of the research projects look, the problems that occurred and how they were overcome. Your students will get the opportunity to ask questions.
- *Part two (afternoon)*: preparing the interview with experts, peers and potential supervisors. We will focus on the preparation of interviews that the students will have as part of their topic exploration. We are asking the students to prepare this part of the session by doing some homework and to interview each other.
- *Part three*: planning the road to the proposal. You will finish this session with a sketch of the different stages of a proposal development and its planning.

3.3 Session 2 part one: Researchers in action

Having listened to the research experiences as presented by two of your colleagues you have invited, the students are challenged to analyse if and how your colleagues have dealt with the essentials of doing research as presented in session one.

Action

Invite your participants to write down their main impressions from your colleagues' introductions. They can use the following checklist for this. They write down their main points in a 5-minute paper. Then you discuss the most important observations in the presence of your colleagues:

- clarity as regards the position of the subject of research in the field of study (embedding in the discipline, engagement with earlier research);
- substantiating that the research problem has not yet been answered satisfactorily;

- proving that answering the research problem is worthwhile in that it contributes to science and/or society (relevance);
- presence of a good leading research question and set of sub-questions;
- the role of propositions, hypotheses or claims in the research;
- well-founded choice in favour of one or more specific research functions: describing, comparing, defining, evaluating, explaining, designing;
- clear definition of the data needed to answer the research question(s);
- well-reasoned choice of methods for the collection of the data.

3.4 Session 2 part two: Interviewing experts, peers and potential supervisors

Organization of this part of the session

This part of the meeting is meant to make students somewhat familiar with interviewing people who can help them explore possible topics for the research proposal to be written later. In preparation, the students read a methodological introduction in semi-structured interviewing, for example, Bryman (2008: Chapter 8) or one of the countless internet sources. This part of the session is completed with the preparation of questions that can be used to interview experts and staff members who can potentially guide the student in developing the research proposal.

Preparatory actions

- You have asked them to bring a set of questions that will lead to in-class interviewing a peer about their strategies in finding a research topic.
- They have also prepared this second session by sending one week before a draft of an email message in which the student invites a scholar, potential supervisor, practitioner or other expert to be interviewed. The student must introduce himself or herself and the aim of the request, next to presenting a limited set of questions to be dealt with in the interview.

Action

In the first part of the afternoon session, the students will practise by interviewing each other about the topic exploration. The students will split up into subgroups, consisting of three persons. They will have 1½ hours for interviewing, being interviewed and observing the interview. You distribute a set of criteria for evaluating the qualities of interviewer and interview (see Appendix L, Section 1). Per half hour the order will be as follows:

A interviews B for 20 minutes. C is the observer and evaluates the interview.

> C will comment on the interview and B can also bring in observations. 10 minutes are available for this evaluation.
>
> After 30 minutes, the interviewing restarts. For example, C interviews A and B will be the evaluator. Because the students all must practise the three distinct roles, they must be strict in keeping to the time schedule.
>
> After 1½ hours, you and the students will start a discussion of the interview with their (potential) supervisor or another expert. The students bring their draft of an email invitation to the session. You will give an introduction of the types of questions that can be asked and the best way to organize the interview.

Collectively, you and the students will check whether their provisional set of questions has the potential to get the best information out of their interviewee.

> **Action**
>
> It works very well to see an interviewer in action. Before or during Session 2, invite one of your students to interview one of their colleagues about the exploration of a topic and the attractiveness of a provisional topic the student has in mind. The other students are the observers and will give feedback (and learn a lot from their courageous fellow students).

Your suggestions for good interviewing

> The interviews contributed the most to my big step forward. Not because the interviewees told me what to do, but because they showed me the weaknesses in my ideas and promoted the good parts.
>
> (former student A.B.)

You start by explaining the function of interviewing others during this topic exploration. Your students will be inspired by meeting the outside world and learning that others are interested in the topics they are considering. Others can confirm the importance of a topic and brainstorm with the interviewer about a 'plan of attack' if several topics are considered. It will teach your students that there are others who are active in their field of interest. In some respects, it can prevent them from 're-inventing the wheel'. They can test the attractiveness of the topics they are considering. You suggest to them also to meet several potential supervisors, without putting the supervision as such on the interview agenda. Your students will discover if there is a clear click between them and a potential supervisor, in terms of personality and substantive interests. If that is the case, they can discuss with you the invitation of that colleague to be their supervisor during the further exploration of the topic and the writing of the research proposal.

Interview guide

Your students have prepared this session by reading a thorough introduction in the art of interviewing. They are aware of the importance of preparing a sound interview guide that will lead them through the interview, in accordance with the goals of the interview.

It will help your students if you are outspoken about the best way to show their eagerness and leadership. They must have a fine feeling for the flow of the interview, the rhythm: formulate leading questions, follow-up questions and probing questions in reserve.

Your most important recommendation: 'You are a passionate young researcher, not a student who must do an assignment.'

You can specify your suggestions because you have read their draft of an email invitation to somebody they want to interview.

> **Possible interview topics**
> - What does your respondent know about your field or topic?
> - What are or have been your respondent's research activities in the field or regarding the topic you are considering?
> - What does the interviewee see as important to research?
> - What does the interviewee expect with respect to topic developments?
> - What does the interviewee want to study?
> - What does the interviewee want a young researcher to research?

- 'Assertiveness or helplessness, that's the question'.
- Show openness in thinking. Invite the interviewee to challenge you.
- Be clear about your earlier topic experiences, the foundations of your interest.
- Show your feeling for discussions among experts.
- Be explicit about the importance of the interviewee.
- In your email invitation, offer to send a set of detailed questions in advance.
- Golden trick: always present a dyad of a question and a 'bid' (for example, a carefully formulated possible answer to your question).
- Formulate a clear position, something you don't know or understand.
- Formulate intriguing issues, puzzles, fascination, research interest.
- Show your familiarity with the publications and the work of your interviewee.
- Show you are starting to get a grip on the literature.
- Formulate complexities and difficulties.
- Formulate a conceptual problem. What would you like to understand better after the research is complete?

You may tell them what you would do if you were in your student's position:

- Make a sharp formulation of what you want to gain from the interview.
- Make yourself familiar with the interviewee (read their publications!) and the literature.
- Do record the interview and make a selective transcription.
- Have a pilot interview with a peer.
- Prepare for unexpected interviewee behaviour. The interviewee might change the roles, asking you: 'What do YOU think about ...?'
- No typing errors in the email. Check the English.
- Start snowballing by asking whom else to contact, what else to read.
- Write a report on the interview and ask the interviewee to check it.
- Do make transcription or report immediately after the interview.
- Make maximum use of the interview while writing a well-reasoned topic choice.

3.5 Session 2 part three: Planning in practice, the 8 months of the proposal preparation

In your introduction, you explain the process-based nature of the development of the proposal:

> **The Proposal as process (taking, for example, 6–8 months)**
> - The proposal will have several versions, several stages.
> - Priority is to start with searching [20] essential texts regarding your provisional topic.
> - Formulate the first version of a leading research question.
> - Search for and read a book about the research design in your discipline.
> - Review the literature you found and develop questions version 2.
> - Do study good practices (proposals written by earlier students).
> - Proposal a quarter of the way: discuss it with peers, supervisors and your Proposal Lab convener.
> - Proposal Halfway, first version, meeting with supervisor.
> - Versions 2 and 3.
> - Handing in final version of Proposal Halfway.
> - Handing in Final Proposal (the 90 per cent okay version).

The participants must not only plan a future PhD trajectory, but also its preparation. The Gantt chart in Figure 4.1 shows an example of the planning of a PhD proposal. This planning assumes that participants also have other (study) activities. If they can work full-time on the proposal, the 8-month period can be reduced. However, it is important that the period contains sufficient moments of reflection and possibilities for revision of the work in progress.

Figure 4.1 Example of a proposal planning (10 months available)

Task	Sept	Oct	Nov	Dec	Jan	Feb	Mar	Apr	May	June
Snapshot	x	x								
Literature search training			x							
Literature search	x	x	x	x	x	x	x			
Literature review				x	x					
Formulating research question, embedded in study of literature				x	x					
Well-reasoned topic choice			x	x						
Literature search report					x	x				
Interviewing experts and writing interview report		x	x	x		x				
Finding supervisors	x	x	x	x						
Meeting supervisors				x	x	x	x	x	x	
Proposal Halfway						x	x	x		
Final proposal									x	x

A special point of attention regarding the literature review. If enough time is taken for this, this not only creates an important building block for the proposal. With a good literature review, an important draft text is written for the future thesis or its components if the PhD candidate starts drafting a thesis based on articles. Of course, this first literature review is a draft. Over the coming years, colleagues will publish articles and books that must be incorporated into an updated version of the literature review.

Explanation

- *The Snapshot*: the document that the participants produce or have already produced in view of the admission to your programme. They outline their initial ideas about a possible investigation. Early in the programme they will discuss this text and the Rough Topic Exploration Matrix (see Session 1 of the Proposal Lab) with you in the first individual feedback meeting.

- *Search training*: education and guidance in finding the most important literature.
- *The literature review*: the text in which the most important literature on the participant's research topic is displayed and critically commented on.
- *Question and embedding*: the formulation of the main question of the research and its relationship with existing scientific insights.
- *Well-reasoned topic choice*: the paper in which the participant makes the subject choice known.
- *Literature search report*: the text in which the participant reports on the search for the most important literature.
- *Interviewing and report*: the participant is motivated to have conversations with experts in the specific field of research during the search process. Based on these discussions, the participant determines which scientists can be the best supervisors for the PhD trajectory (*Finding a supervisor*). It is therefore not assumed that these supervisors are there from the very beginning. As soon as the participant and supervisor(s) have found each other, the supervisor will naturally play a crucial role in the further development of the research ideas.
- *Proposal Halfway*: approximately halfway, the participant writes the first fully-fledged draft of a proposal for the doctoral research. This is the subject of feedback from fellow Proposal Lab participants, the Lab convener, and the potential supervisors of the PhD research.

Action

After you have explained the importance of planning and presented the planning of activities in the coming year, you invite your students to do an exercise in planning, leading to a well-reasoned topic choice. The activities figure in the Gantt chart that you will find in Appendix F, Table 6.4.

3.6 Post-session assignment: two interviews and two interview reports

Action

The students will interview two experienced researchers about their topic. One of them might be their future supervisor. Explain to your students that in the interview they should avoid talking about the possibility of the interviewee becoming their supervisors of the project. One of the functions of the interview is to see if there is a click between the interviewer and the possible supervisor. If this proves not to be the case and the supervision has already been the subject of discussion, it is extremely difficult for the student to retract the suggestion.

> **Action**
>
> Your students will write a report on at least two of the interviews they will have. The components of the report are:
>
> 1. The two interview guides (maximum two pages in total).
> 2. Two brief reports on the substance, the major results, of the interviews (maximum two x three pages.).
> 3. Two notes on how the interviews went, where they took place and whether they opened new avenues of interest.
>
> The students will send you the interview report ultimately [to be decided by the convener]. You can read the details of the report format and suggestions for evaluating an interview report in Appendix L, Section 1.

3.7 Literature suggestions

Bryman (2008: Chapter 18), 'Interviewing in qualitative research'.
Gosling and Noordam (2006: Chapter 6), 'Charting your progress month by month'.

4 Session 3: the PhD proposal

4.1 Script for Session 3

Pre-session activities

Reading Brewer (2007: 79–93): 'The Research Proposal'.
Reading Watts (2001): 'The Holy Grail: In Pursuit of the Dissertation Proposal'.
Reading two proposals, written by predecessors.
Reading rubrics for the evaluation of proposals (see Appendix G, Section 2).

Introducing the research proposal and its quality criteria

Early in the programme we will discuss in detail what the result of the students' work should look like. All sections of the proposal are related to the parts of our programme. In the first meeting we gave a brief introduction to the proposal. In Session 3 we go into the details.

The explanation of the proposal format functions as a map, as a compass. The explanation shows the context of everything we are going to teach the students. Brewer's (2007) chapter on the Research Proposal is a good introduction. He also makes an interesting suggestion that you can consider. In addition to the proposal, he suggests providing an overview of the chapters the student expects to be contained in the thesis.

In this third session we will discuss the components of the proposal in detail, next to an explanation of the quality criteria that will apply. It may be best to explain the proposal early in the programme but return to it once the actual writing has started and implementation issues can be discussed.

In-session activity

After this introduction, the students will discuss two proposals sent to them before the session. They will do so based on the quality criteria – the rubrics – they also have received earlier.

4.2 Your explanation of the components of a PhD proposal

See Appendix I where this proposal information is presented in form format.

1. *Title of the research project*
2. The *abstract:* Usually, this part of a proposal is called The Abstract. In this case, it should be between 200 and 250 words long (usually 100–150 words), or as short as possible without omitting essential information or endangering its accuracy. It should state:
   - what is presented, theorized, studied;
   - the purpose and context of the research;
   - theories used to explain what will be reported;
   - the hypotheses, which will be evaluated, and/or the leading research question and the sub-questions which the research project will attempt to answer;
   - what the sample(s) or units/subjects of study will be;
   - how data will be collected and analysed (the research methods used);
   - the relevance of the research project to the field of study.
3. *The research question*
   a. Description of the field of study and the existing body of knowledge with reference to that. What don't we know and understand? What has been neglected? What is the central object of the proposed research? And what is the research objective? You challenge your students to try as hard as they can to formulate their research interests in terms of a conceptual problem, in terms of what we do not know or understand, in terms of something that we want to make understandable for others.

> **Explanation**
>
> This part of the proposal is directly inspired by what the students have read in the literature, the interviews they held, the meetings they had with their (possible) supervisor, and what they will write down in the Critical Appraisal Assignment (Session 6 and Appendix L, Section 3) and Question Practicum (see Appendix K). The processing of all this information will have a place in their well-reasoned topic choice. Your students can be sure that those texts contain sentences they are pleased with, expressing exactly where they want to focus on.

b. The core question. Which central question would your student like to answer with the research? How does he or she unfold the central question into sub-questions, so that the joint answers will generate the answer to the central question?

> **Explanation**
>
> Let the students start with their research objective, for which purpose they will gather and analyse the data. Next, make them take provisional decisions about the type of research questions they want to answer (in correspondence with the research objective). Remember the core qualities of good questions as explained by Bryman (2008):
>
> - The question must be clear, researchable.
> - There should be literature on which you can draw to help illuminate how your research question should be approached.
> - There is the prospect of being able to make a contribution – however small – to the field of expertise on the topic.
> - It should be neither too broad nor too narrow.
>
> The questions should have a steering function, indicating what different types of knowledge are required and what material needs to be gathered (Verschuren and Doorewaard, 2005).

4 *The innovative character of the proposed project*
What is the significance of the proposed research? Does it contain an original contribution to the field of existing knowledge? Is it of specific social or theoretical relevance?

5 *Considerations regarding theory and prior empirical research*
Sketch of the *dominant theoretical approaches* and debates. Sketch of the *dominant empirical findings*. How does your student's research fit in with the present state of research and theoretical discussions in your field? Which scholars are especially relevant to your student's work?

The foundation for all this information is lying in the student's literature search, literature notes, critical appraisal and literature review, for example:

> In view of this assignment, I used the following working definition of theory. 'A theory is a collection of well-motivated, disciplinary, embedded and researchable propositions/theses that try to explain or try to understand, for example, the existence or non-existence of ..., the similarities and differences between A&B ..., the (in)effectiveness of a ..., the plausibility of a future development, etc.'

6 *Proposition, hypotheses and concepts*
What is the central proposition? Your argument? What are the working hypotheses? What are the main theoretical concepts you intend to use?

> **Explanation**
>
> In this part of the proposal, your students formulate their propositions and hypotheses they want to evaluate in their project.
>
> Think of Turabian (2007: 50), who describes the initial stages of research as finding a question and imagining a tentative answer, i.e., the working hypothesis.
>
> Or look at the definition given in the *Oxford Dictionary of Psychology* (Colman, 2009): 'Hypothesis. A tentative explanation for a phenomenon, subject to criticism by rational argument and refutation by empirical evidence.'
>
> And, especially, read the very inspiring chapters by Booth et al. (2016) on 'Making Good Arguments and Making Claims'.
>
> It is important to recognize that research does not always have to be based on theoretical assumptions, (working) hypotheses or claims. The research can also aim to formulate a theory based on empirical material. Such an approach was developed in the social sciences by Glaser and Strauss (2009) via the method of the so-called Grounded Theory.

7 *The data and methods*
In this part of the proposal, the empirical data, the sources, the documents to be used to answer each of the research questions are mentioned. How do your students intend to gather their data? Do they have whatever permission might be required? Have the necessary informants agreed to co-operate? Do they have access to the sources they need?

We finish this information about what we expect halfway through the programme with some strategic suggestions for the students.

"Provide concise and clear answers, based on the ideas and information you have halfway on the journey to a PhD Proposal, i.e. the Proposal Halfway. If new data and theoretical insights become available, you may have other ideas and your plans may change accordingly. We will discuss your Proposal Halfway in a face-to-face meeting. After another 3 months you will hand in the Final Proposal".

8 *The planning of the 4 year dissertation project*
In some situations, the candidates are asked to enclose with the proposal a schedule for the 4 years that a PhD project usually takes. The participants in the

Proposal Lab or the individual proposal preparers can use two appendices for this purpose: Appendix O. 'Planning matrix PhD trajectory (research and other activities)'; and Appendix N. 'Expectations in View of a 4 Year PhD Project'.

The overview has been composed based on advice by supervisors working in the technical and educational disciplines. It must be adapted to the requirements of your own discipline and field of research.

4.3 Quality criteria that will apply to the Proposal Halfway and the Final Proposal

Appendix G contains the rubrics that are helpful to students in getting a grasp on the criteria that apply to the assessment of a PhD proposal and the result of a PhD trajectory, the thesis.

We worked in our Proposal Lab with rubrics such as those developed in 2007 by our colleague Heinze Oost and elaborated by Rob van Gestel and Hans Sonneveld.

4.4 special case: originality and relevance

Thesis plans will be assessed on several qualities by future supervisors, admission committees or committees that award subsidies. In *What is Originality in the Humanities and the Social Sciences?* Guetzkow, Lamont and Mallard (2004) show what the dominant assessment criteria are in the committees that must assess research proposals. Their research focused on the humanities and social sciences. However, the results of this research also apply to other disciplines. In their research, six criteria turned out to be dominant in the quality assessment of a research proposal: (1) clarity; (2) 'quality' (in all its different operationalizations); (3) originality; (4) significance; (5) methods; and (6) feasibility.

In one part of your programme, you will pay attention to the originality of the thesis plan your students are developing. This criterion is often one they fear. By intuition, they feel that in a PhD project the evaluators of their proposal often will judge their plans on this criterion. Your students blow this criterion up to mythological proportions and have no idea how to give it hands and feet. The research of Guetzkow et al. (2004) can bring a lot of peace and allay the students' fears. These authors show that in the assessors' practice many definitions of originality arise. In an overview they show 28 types of originality. They distinguish seven main types of originality that can be operationalized further: (1) an original approach; (2) an understudied area; (3) an original topic; (4) an original theory; (5) an original method; (6) original data; and (7) original results (ibid.: 197).

Your students can specify these main types of originality by asking themselves questions such as: will I formulate new questions? Will I study aspects of my topic that have been understudied until now? Will I bring together theoretical insights in an unexpected way? Will I combine methods in an unexpected way? Most likely, their topic is already original just because they will be collecting new data and providing new insights.

Explain to your participants that supervisors can have a one-sided perspective on what constitutes an original study. For example, they may be of the opinion that originality must always be linked to new theoretical insights and have an insufficient eye for originality in the form of researching an understudied sector or subject with existing theoretical insights.

> **Action**
>
> After your introduction and explanation of this criterion, you can ask your students to indicate in which respect their topic might be original. The overview of Guetzkow et al. (2004) can help them answer that question. Invite them to read their article, available on the internet as an open-source document:
>   (https://www.researchgate.net/publication/241644109_What_Is_Originality_in_the_Social_Sciences_and_the_Humanities).
>   It makes sense to discuss this aspect of the forthcoming proposal again after they have got a grip on the literature available on their subject.
>   In this context, it may also be useful to address the issue of the relevance of the proposed research: the consequences in terms of understanding a phenomenon or its societal consequences, and its impact on our academic world and the broader world around us.
>   It is best to discuss again originality and relevance with the students after the sessions on the literature search and literature review and before submitting the proposal halfway. Then they will be more capable of evaluating their own subject in the making against the different definitions of originality and relevance.

4.5 Application of insights, in-session assignment

Two weeks before this meeting, you will have sent your students the Appendix G 'Rubrics for evaluating the proposal qualities' and two proposals, written by earlier participants in your programme.

> **Action**
>
> You invite the students to discuss the qualities of the proposals in sub-groups and to report their main conclusion in the plenary session.

4.6 Post-session assignment

Your participants write a reflection paper on the implications of the literature study, your introductions, proposals they have read, and what they have heard from colleagues for themselves and the deliberations with their supervisor. They will send you a copy of this reflection paper for feedback.

5 Session 4: searching for the important literature

5.1 Introduction

Much of the topic exploration deals with written sources. Which researchers have made the trip in this area before? What have they written about it? What were their main findings? And what suggestions for research do they make? The participants in your Proposal Lab will be aware of their closest colleagues, get a grip on what is already known and develop a feeling for the hot issues in their research niche. The central question is whether the students will be able to substantiate the importance of their research in the proposal.

Finding the most important literature is a dialectical process. The students will start with an embryonic research interest, will search for the associated literature, and will subsequently adjust or drop the subject and will again search for literature and start the cycle again.

5.2 Script of the session

Part one (morning)

- introduction of quality criteria that apply to positioning oneself within the discipline;
- introduction to literature search strategies by you or librarians in your faculty;
- report by a PhD candidate on their literature search experiences;
- practice in literature search.

Part two (afternoon)

- introduction of the most important principles of engaging the existing knowledge;
- discussion of The Disciplinary Embedding Assignment (see Appendix J on p. 184);
- discussion of two thesis summaries, with a focus on evaluating the quality of the disciplinary embedding.

5.3 Pre-session assignment and preparation

Reading before the fourth meeting: the literature

Aveyard (2007: Chapters 1–4). These chapters deal with topics such as:

- Why do a literature review?
- Determining which literature is important for the student's project.
- The connection between research question and literature search.
- How to search for the literature.

One of the most important messages from Aveyard's book can be a great comfort to your students: it is important to have a research question that is neither too comprehensive nor too restricted:

> Ideally you will retrieve 10–20 references that are well focused on your topic … It would be difficult to address your research question with fewer references, but you would be inundated with literature if many more references were identified.
>
> (Aveyard 2008: 66)

Reading before the fourth meeting

Two thesis summaries

Pre-session literature search assignment

You show your students the way to the websites leading to the most important journals in view of their research.

> **Action**
>
> You ask them to prepare individually a brief note (Appendix J, The Disciplinary Embedding Assignment) containing the following information:
>
> - formulation of their provisional research topic;
> - an overview of journals they wish to consult with respect to their research topic, mentioning the title of the journals and the motivation of their choice;
> - any problems they have met in this exercise.
>
> Make them aware of the fact that journals in other languages than English are also an option, and do not forget journals in other disciplines.
>
> Let them send this note to the library specialists and to you, some days before the fourth meeting. See Section 5.5 of this session for more information.

5.4 Your introduction: quality criteria that apply to the literature review

Before introducing the literature search strategies, you contextualize them by introducing the criteria that will be used by the reviewers of the proposal.

Here you will find the rubric formulated in view of the positioning of one's research within the discipline.

> **Rubric**
>
> Rubric for the argument for the newsworthiness, theoretical and/or practical or social relevance, and scope of the research problem (originality, relevance).
>
> 1= Lack of justification/justification section lacking an arguable position in outline.
> 2= Justification arguing for the newsworthiness and relevance of the research problem, needing greater care in documenting sources, greater effort in organizing the text and/or a deeper level of analysis.
> 3= Selective literature review adequately substantiating that the research problem has not yet been answered sufficiently (newsworthiness) and contributes to science (theoretical relevance) and/or society (practical/social relevance). Information on the scope of the research problem may be limited.
> 4= Selective and critical literature review effectively substantiating that the research problem has not yet been answered sufficiently (newsworthiness) and contributes to science (theoretical relevance) and/or society (practical/social relevance). Information on the scope of the research problem may be limited.
> 5= Selective and critical literature review effectively substantiating that the research problem has not yet been answered sufficiently (newsworthiness), contributes to science (theoretical relevance) and/or society (practical/social relevance), and cannot yield more information, given the subject, conditions and the research context (scope). Clear information on the scope of the research, clearly showing 'the bigger story' behind the specific topic.

5.5 Introduction and practicum in search strategies: part one of Session 4

Introduction part one: the library specialists

Preferably, this part of the session is organized by you in collaboration with specialists from your library who have a good grip on the relevant literature for your students and have considerable expertise in doing a literature search. The library specialists start with an explanation of the most important aspects of a literature search and their observations vis-à-vis the notes sent by the students to the librarians and the Lab convener. Components of the introduction are:

- knowing the importance of a systematic approach to the literature review;
- distinguishing several alternative methods of searching the literature:

- snowball sampling: finding literature by using a key document as a starting point, consulting the bibliography in the key document (book or journal article) to find other relevant titles, and again studying the bibliographies of these new publications to find more relevant titles;
  - scrutinizing reference lists of key articles;
  - author searching.
- recording the search strategy and writing down the strengths and limitations of the strategy;
- reading abstracts to identify the relevance of an article or book;
- knowing the principles of a critical appraisal of the literature found.

Introduction part two: the fellow PhD candidate

We can facilitate the transition from expert information to application by having a PhD candidate, who previously has attended our programme, report on the experiences with the literature search. Marnix was close to our participants, and they did not shy away from asking questions that they thought were 'stupid'. He illustrated his literature search experiences with his own uncertainties, crashes and successes within the context of a research project that came close to the students' interests. He was one of them.

Literature search in practice

Action

After this introduction, the meeting turns into a practicum. The students will open the journal websites and apply the search principles that have been explained by you or the librarians, in combination with the insights they gained by reading the relevant literature. This part of the meeting ends with an exchange of experiences and questions answered by you or the librarians.

5.6 Disciplinary embedding and engaging the literature: part two of Session 4

Preparatory practical exercise by the students

Ideally, this second part of Session 4 starts after a break upon finishing the morning session. This applies to a one-day programme during which both the search techniques and the issue of disciplinary embedding are dealt with. Of course, you may decide to spread these topics over two days.

Students have prepared this part of the session by way of some homework. They have sent the results of their homework to you before the meeting. This will enable you to get a grip on any problems they have found. The instruction reads as follows (see Appendix J):

In preparation for the session on Disciplinary Embedding, you will write down your research area, a specific research theme and your provisional research topic. In this assignment, we ask you to try and fill out a complete 'specification'. Please write down your specification on this form. Try to follow the specification steps of:

- discipline;
- disciplinary sub-field;
- your theme;
- essential 'others' (fellow researchers);
- their debates;
- remaining questions (in your view, in the opinion of other authors);
- your niche for doing something relevant, original;
- theoretical anchor points, as offered by other authors;
- your subject.

If your subject is located at the meeting point of several disciplines, first clarify which disciplines are involved and how your research is anchored in those disciplines. If you will be working in more than one discipline, you will do the specification two times. Find out if researchers work at the meeting point of two or more disciplines on a subject that overlaps with your own interest.

We realize that the following subjects can lead to headaches:

- the debates of essential others (in view of your research theme or topic), their creative agreements, their creative disagreements ...);
- their theories (theoretical, analytical, interpretative, explanatory frameworks) of relevance for the theme under study;
- remaining questions, research issues (in your view, in the opinion of other authors).

You may keep these in reserve for our meeting a couple of months later when we will discuss your well-reasoned topic choice. But if you dare to give it a try already now, we will gladly give feedback!

Preparatory reading by the students

Before the meeting, you have invited your students to read some texts. First, there are two chapters in Booth et al. (2016): Chapter 5, 'From Problems to Sources' and Chapter 6, 'Engaging the Sources'. It is wise to discuss the main points of Booth or a similar text with your students in your own introduction.

You have sent your students the summaries of two theses that have been defended successfully and the rubrics for evaluating the strengths and weaknesses of the literature review (see Appendix J, 'The Disciplinary Embedding Assignment'). You have invited them to evaluate these summaries and to bring their main conclusions to the meeting.

In-session activities

You start the session with your introduction of the most important principles of engaging the existing knowledge. Below you will find some building blocks I always incorporated in my own teaching.

Zooming in

Initially, students will encounter a multitude of articles and books in their literature search. An important aspect of the search is an increasingly sharp focus on the small group of texts and authors that are relevant to the student's research. We will arrive at the 15–20 texts and authors predicted by Aveyard (2008).

> **Zooming in**
> - Searching and selecting essential journals and books from your total reading list.
> - Finding 15–20 essential texts.
> - Critically appraising these articles and books.
> - Try out: Writing an extract of a literature review (based on five texts).
> - Writing a condensed version of the review, as part of the research proposal.

The essentials of disciplinary embedding

You explain to your students why a good literature review is so important for a good research design. The researchers become aware of their closest colleagues, get a grip on what is already known and develop a feeling for the hot issues in this research niche. In our Proposal Lab we try to make the student develop a starting point, a question in which the student is interested, as early as possible.

We do not offer the students a poisoned cup by letting them read mountains of literature at random. On the contrary, the student starts with a roadmap, a compass, a direction ... which is refined and adjusted while studying. This means that we question the students about this initial interest upon admission to the programme. 'I just enjoy doing research, but I don't know yet on what' is not a basis for participation in the Proposal Lab.

This approach is in line with Craig Loehle's advice (Loehle, 2010):

- Work on your idea first, then compare it to the existing literature;

as opposed to:

- desperately seeking a topic in the literature.

What your students produce during your programme will be of great value when it comes to a PhD project. The definitive version of their review, supplemented and amended, will be used in their thesis. In a thesis, there are several options for positioning the literature review: (1) as part of an extensive introduction; (2) as a separate chapter; (3) as a starting paragraph of each chapter, especially in the case of a thesis based on articles.

> **The essence of the theoretical embedding**
>
> - Specifying the discipline(s) in which you are working
> - Finding out which scientists are working in your field
> - Finding out which scientists are in conversation with each other (a creative agreement or disagreement, or a debate regarding your topic)
> - Finding out which theoretical framework is most suitable for your theoretical analysis of the subject
> - The development of theoretical/interpretative/analytical propositions that will lead your research

Using secondary sources

Again, the work of Booth (Booth et al., 2016: Chapter 6, 'Engaging sources') can be a major source of inspiration. In summary, he suggests the following approaches I always presented in my own introductions on this topic:

1. Using sources for creative agreement:
   - Offering additional support to a source's claim.
   - Confirming unsupported claims.
   - Applying a claim more widely.
2. Looking for creative disagreement:
   - Challenging that x is a kind of y.
   - Showing that source mistakes can be made in the following:
     - how parts of something are related;
     - the origin and development of a topic;
     - a causal relationship.
   - Contradicting a standard view of things, urging others to think in a new way.

After your introduction, you will discuss with the students the results of their pre-session Embedding and Relevance Assignment.

Often, we learn a lot from evaluating others' work. This will be the crucial point in part three of this afternoon's session. You will split up your group of students into three sub-groups to discuss the value of the thesis summaries by x and y. Each sub-group will grade the two thesis summaries, making use of the rubric for evaluating disciplinary embedding and relevance (see the rubric earlier in this session overview and Appendix J). You will bring together the sub-groups' conclusions. As you can see, in our programme we familiarize students with studying a thesis as soon as possible. I once organized a programme for first-year PhD candidates. I asked them which of them had ever seen a thesis. Half replied in the affirmative. Such unfamiliarity contributes to the mythology of the PhD thesis.

At the end of this day, we will ask our students to formulate their main intentions in view of further action regarding disciplinary embedding and engaging the sources.

5.7 Post-session assignment

Literature search report

Your students will write a report on their literature search. You explain to them the format of such a report (see Appendix L, 'Evaluation of the literature search report' on p. 189).

Here is the generic format for a literature search report:

1 Introduction of major research questions that have guided the search process.
2 Preparation of the literature search:
   - keywords, search terms and synonyms;
   - databases;
   - deciding on inclusion and exclusion criteria (which sources to use, which not to use).
3 The literature search in action – the sources we did consult:
   - electronic databases;
   - reference list searching ('snowballing');
   - talking to experts.
4 Judging the relevance of the publications.
5 The way the results of the literature search are stored.
6 The strengths and limitations of the way the search process has been performed.
7 A short conclusion (which major problems have been encountered, how they have been solved, lessons for future search actions).

Annex 1: Keywords, search terms.
Annex 2: Key references (the 20 most important documents found by the literature search).

6 Session 5: the literature review

This is a labour-intensive and long session. The students will have to preparatory work. During the meeting they will also conduct practical assignments that promote mutual communication.

6.1 Preparatory activities

In view of this fifth session, you invite your students by email:

1 To read Aveyard's (2008) chapters; 'How do I critically appraise the literature?', 'How do I synthesize my findings?', 'Why do a literature review?' and 'How do I present my literature review?', or a similar text that covers these topics.
2 To read Booth et al. (2016: Chapter 6), 'Taking notes'.
3 To write a brief report on their own style of note-taking (to be discussed pairwise during the session).
4 To read the 'Evaluation of the critical appraisals' form (see Appendix L, Section 3, on p. 191).
5 To take two copies to the session of articles they have read carefully and to write down critical observations in view of those articles (using Appendix L, 'Evaluation of the critical appraisals') and the major themes the articles deal with, with special attention to which themes they share.
6 To read a good literature review (sent to them by you with the email), preferably written by an earlier participant in your Proposal Lab, or an earlier PhD candidate

6.2 Programme

1 Your introduction of the literature review: 'The bigger picture of this session'.
2 Note-taking:
   a Your presentation: 'Golden rules for note-taking'.
   b Invite your students to organize individually the main findings from the two articles they have read in a chart like Figure 4.2. (This overview is based on Aveyard (2008: 112). I added the column 'Most important key words resulting from your coding').
   c Evaluate their experiences in a plenary.
3 Critical appraisal:
   a Your presentation: 'The essence of a critical appraisal'.
   b Inventory of critical appraisal experiences in view of the two articles read in preparation of this session (plenary).
4 Literature review:
   a Your introduction: 'The essence of a good literature review'.

Figure 4.2 Overview chart of literature read

Author/ date	Most important key words resulting from your coding	Aim of study/ paper	Type of study/ information	Main findings/ conclusions	Strengths and limitations
Publication 1					
Publication 2, etc.					

b Discussing a good example of a literature review (plenary).
c In four sub-groups: 'On the way to my literature review: the essentials'. What are the main lessons they take from this session?
d Brief presentations by the sub-groups.

6.3 Your introduction of the literature review, the bigger picture of this session

The literature review is an important building block in every proposal. In your introduction you present the key features of a literature review. You also explain what it is NOT: not a list of authors and their work, in the order in which your student has read the texts. The main purpose of the review is that your students can position their own plans in relation to existing knowledge.

You also explain the study techniques that form the basis of a good review. Earlier you discussed the first step: the development of good search strategies. The second consists of the student making systematic notes of the text studied. Third, it concerns the critical appraisal of the text.

Below we will take a closer look at taking notes, the critical appraisal of texts and the structure of a review. Again, we do not assume that your students already have these basic skills. Obviously, this applies to Master's students from your own faculty, but caution is also required with PhD candidates. Think, for example, of international candidates who have been trained elsewhere. However, if it turns out that you are treading well-trodden paths on these parts, you can be brief here. But check whether all your participants have mastered these techniques.

So, what is a good review and what is it not? It is essential for positioning your plans in the specific field of study. Bryman (2008) summarizes the main functions of a literature review. Writing a literature review will help you to find out the following:

1 What is already known about this area – locating your research in a theoretical context

2 The current debates, theories and relevant concepts
3 The research methods that have been used
4 Gaps, inconsistencies, and unanswered questions
5 Your analytical framework
6 Variables to include in your research that you might not otherwise thought about

You must explain what a literature review is not! It is not a summing up of authors and titles, building up a position by choosing a sample of texts that do not represent the breadth of perspectives, only presenting comfortable examples and avoiding authors who do not support your argument.

You also explain the structure of a review to your participants. See also Section 6.8, information for the students regarding the extract of the literature review.

6.4 Explanation of the literature review quality criteria

You distribute Appendix L, Section 4, 'Evaluation of a literature review' and discuss the details.

6.5 Basic technique for a review: the notes

Before you formulate your recommendations, you invite your participants to talk about their own experiences in note-taking. Ask them to formulate their experiences in terms of SWOT analysis, Strengths, Weaknesses, Opportunities and Threats. Write down their major observations on the blackboard to track down lines and patterns.

Then, you explain the characteristics of taking notes.

1 What is a note?
   a A short written text, related to a source, dealing with its words and ideas, and its implications, consequences, shortcomings, and new possibilities.
2 The goals:
   a Collecting and writing down information for a critical appraisal and the literature review.
   b Facilitating the development of your own ideas.
3 The necessary conditions:
   a An open mind. Avoid just picking the information that suits you.
   b Storing: build a data set of notes; this will save a lot of time and prevents you from just relying on your memory.
4 The substance of a note is bibliographic data: standardized substantive notes contain information (see Turabian, 2007: 36–47) on the following:
   a The major argument of the author, findings, and data.

b Your own response: agreement, disagreement, value in view of your question.
c Reasons that support your hypothesis or suggest a new one.
d Evidence that supports your presumptions.
e Views that undermine or even contradict your presumptions, your hypothesis.
f Historical background of your question.
g Historical or contemporary context, explaining the importance of your question.
h Important definitions.
i The keywords you have written down in the margin of the text.

Use keywords! Encode your texts! After having made several notes, you will be able to compare the notes (thus: the texts) by analysing your information per keyword. You will discover themes they share, either by agreement or disagreement; you will also recognize texts that are outliers. This is an essential step in the synthesizing of your findings into a review and getting a grip on the discussions regarding their topic. Your students can summarize their notes in an overview that can look like Figure 4.2.

> **Action**
>
> Invite your students to organize in class the main findings from the two articles they have read in a chart like Figure 4.2.

6.6 Basic technique for a review: the critical appraisal of the text

The next step towards the literature review consists of the critical assessment of the books, articles and papers read. The critical appraisal of the literature lays the foundation for arguing the strengths and weaknesses of a publication. Students can prepare for this by assessing two articles based on the checklist as mentioned in Appendix L, Section 3.

In her book, Greenhalgh (2010) includes several checklists that are helpful in analysing scientific texts. Although her book focuses on evidence-based medicine, scattered throughout the text are numerous checkpoints that are also useful for the assessment of scientific work in other disciplines. Based on this important work, I was able to create a checklist for reviewing publications in completely different disciplines. You will find the details in Appendix L, Section 3. It contains the elaborated checkpoints:

- to determine what the publication is about;
- for the methods section of the paper;

- for the robustness of the publication;
- for evaluating the results;
- for further research.

6.7 Synthesizing the findings: the literature review

In your introduction, you present the most important aspects of a literature review:

1. Introduction of the research that makes up the context of the literature review:
   - presentation of research questions that lead the literature review;
   - showing the importance of the review and why the reader needs to read it and offer a road map for the reader of the literature review.
2. The literature review should meet the following criteria:
   - It is comprehensive and up to date.
   - It shows critical and analytical thinking about the literature, so not just a summary of what is read; it shows the strenghts and limitations of the literature.
   - It shows command of the literature.
   - It is selective by discriminating between important and unimportant works.
   - It is based on thematic structuring: per paragraph it brings together authors vis-à-vis themes they discuss. It is not a presentation of authors presented in the consecutive order of reading.
   - It shows a clear alignment with the research questions.
3. The conclusion of the review performs the following functions:
   - It summarizes the main findings.
   - It refers back to the introduction.
   - It ties everything together.
   - It shows the implications for the author's research, for example, by adjusting the research questions.

One of our concluding suggestions emphasizes the composition of the review: the text is broken up into paragraphs with thematic sub-headings.

> **Action**
>
> During this meeting, you invite your students to evaluate a literature review written by a participant in an earlier version of your programme or a PhD candidate. You have sent this review to them some time before the session, together with Appendix L, Section 4.

6.8 Post-session assignment: writing an extract of a literature review

Post-session, students will review five articles in their field of research from a peer review perspective and will write a trial version of a literature review. They will indicate:

- the strong and weak aspects of the work in question in terms of quality and methodology;
- the type of research that is used;
- whether there is a sharp problem formulation and a clear research question;
- whether the research question is answered.

They will depart from the knowledge acquired in this session on 'writing a critical appraisal' and make use of the quality criteria mentioned in Appendix L, Sections 3 and 4.

Submission date: about 6 weeks after this session.

> **Action**
>
> "Consult Aveyard (2007: Chapter 8), or a comparable guide in your discipline for a suggested structure of the literature review. You may limit yourself to the Aveyard items: Title Page, Contents Page, Introduction, Results, Discussion, References. And do not forget her 'Top tips for writing up your literature review'. Also refer to Appendix L, Section 4 for detailed information on the structure."

7 The second individual feedback meeting: the well-reasoned topic choice

7.1 The assignment

At about two and a half months after the start of the programme, your students will complete their 'topic exploration'. They write a paper entitled 'A well-reasoned topic choice'. This paper has the following components:

1 An Introduction containing information on:
   a the importance for the author of the topic exploration;
   b the way in which the author has come to the choice of topics which have been researched in detail;
   c the sources that were used for the exploration of the topics.
2 The approach of the 'topic exploration' and the evaluation of the approach: what went well, where did they meet problems, how did they solve them?

3 What do five obvious 'sources of inspiration' tell the author about the possible topics?
   a previous study and research activities of the author;
   b experts, possible supervisors, peers, etc;
   c the literature;
   d studied case material and examples, (social) experiences of the author;
   e the 'research file' of the author.
4 A comparative strength/weakness analysis of the various topics that the author has examined and considered.
5 Conclusion:
   a Which topic does the author choose after careful consideration? (This choice reflects the ideas and thinking at this moment of writing. In the months that will follow, the ideas might change. That is a natural thing.)
   b The function of the topic choice and subsequent proposal: will it be developed in view of a Master's thesis, or PhD proposal, or application for an internal or external PhD position, or as a 'stand-alone' exercise in writing a proposal?
   c The location of the execution of the research.
   d Supervision: who can supervise and advise the author in the process of proposal writing?
   e Issues that are still open, points which the author wishes to discuss with the convener of the Proposal Lab and supervisors.
6 Bibliography: the paper (2500–3000 words) contains a bibliography of 20 texts (articles, book chapters, books) the author considers to be closely related to the topic.

7.2 The feedback on the well-reasoned topic choice

You will discuss the well-reasoned topic choice with the participants in the Proposal Lab during an individual meeting. You can expect the following topics to be addressed:

- the value of the topic exploration as such;
- the topic exploration requires a new way of studying;
- how both reason and intuition play an important role;
- the experience of uncertainties and how to deal with them;
- stages in the topic exploration;
- how the students also develop their own exploration techniques;
- the great importance of a thorough exploration of the literature;
- moments of break-through are there, it is not only a continuous process of making progress;

- a big step forward: contact with a possible supervisor and interviewing the experts;
- learning a lot from your fellow students;
- work to be done: sharper research questions;
- the wish to understand and to explain is there.

8 Session 6: from topic to questions

By this time, students have been orienting more narrowly towards a particular research topic. In this session, students will learn how to formulate research questions about a topic. The different types of research questions will be dealt with. After the introductory part of the session, the participants will offer feedback to each other on work sent around earlier. You finish the sessions with your main observations and suggestions in response to the Questions Practicums you read.

8.1 Preparation of the session by your students

Exercise in formulating types of questions

In preparation for this meeting, we invite the students to formulate their subject in different types of questions. It is a brain exercise for questioning the subject of preference in different ways. We formulate our invitation to join The Question Practicum (Appendix K) as follows:

> You have reached the moment it will be possible to transform your major interest in a topic into several question options. Try to write down your interest (or aspects of it) in the format of each of the six question options. For example: if my research preference would be a descriptive one, my leading research question could read as follows [..........], and my sub-questions as follows [1..........2..........3......]. Do not panic if an option doesn't link up with your interest or the intrinsic qualities of the topic. If a type really does not fit your research objective, leave it out.
>
> If you hesitate regarding several topics, just choose one to do this exercise in question gymnastics. Send this Assignment to your peer (see scheme – [to be composed by the convener]), and the convener(s) of the programme ultimately 3 days before our sixth meeting.
>
> The goal of this exercise is to let you 'play' with different question type options. At the end, you will have to decide which question type and research perspective you feel most comfortable with and is most appropriate in view of your research goal. One tip: do not think in mutually exclusive question options. For example, whatever your ultimate research objective might be, descriptive questions will always figure somewhere in your overview of main question and sub-questions.

Preparatory reading

Booth et al. (2016: Chapter 3), 'From topic to questions'.
Meltzoff (2007: Chapter 2), 'Research questions and hypotheses'.

8.2 Suggestions for your introduction

From topic to question

Our students have now mapped their research interests and carefully taken steps towards a specific topic. The next step is to translate the interest in a subject into a research question. This is often an overarching question that we can only answer by answering several sub-questions.

Types of questions

Which types of question can we distinguish?

- *Existence questions*: 'Does x exist?' Important when existence or nonexistence of something is controversial (Meltzoff, 2007).
- *Questions of description, classification and composition*: 'What is x like? Is it variable or invariant? ... What are the components that make up x?' (Meltzoff, 2007). 'What are its qualities, what characteristics does it have? How is it? What is it made of? Who or what does it involve? What are the most important steps? What does it look like?' (Oost, 2003).
- *Descriptive-comparative questions*: 'What are the differences? What are the similarities? In what ways are they different? In what ways do they overlap, are they the same?' (Oost, 2003).
- *Relationship questions*: 'Is there a relationship between x and y?' (Meltzoff, 2007).
- *Causality questions*: 'Does x cause, lead to, or prevent changes in y?' (Meltzoff, 2007). 'Why is it so? How did it happen? What is this a consequence of? What reasons are there? What is its background? How could this happen?' (Oost, 2003).
- *Questions of evaluation*: 'How well does it work? ... What are its advantages and disadvantages?' (Meltzoff, 2007).

Evaluating the quality of questions

According to Bryman (2008: 74), the research questions for a thesis or project:

- Should be clear.
- Should be researchable: They should be capable of development into a research design, so that data may be collected in relation to them. This means that extremely abstract terms are unlikely to be suitable.
- Should connect with established theory and research.

- Should be linked with each other: It is especially useful to see the research questions as a pyramid with several layers. On top is the leading research question of the research; layer two consists of the sub-questions to answer the leading questions. Layer three consists of sub-sub-questions you need to answer on behalf of the specific sub-questions. Delete any question that is not essential for answering the main question of the study.
- Should have potential for contributing to knowledge.
- Should be neither too broad nor too narrow.

Booth et al. (2008) also offer useful advice on what to avoid:

- Questions whose answers are settled fact you could just look up.
- Questions that will not be answerable; where it is impossible to find hard data that might settle the question.
- Questions that are based on preference.
- Questions that make you read too many sources.
- Questions for which you cannot find the sources.
- Questions whose answer you cannot disprove.

I conclude with the rubric for evaluating the qualities of research questions (see also Appendix G, Section 3).

Rubric

Research problem (formulating the most important question the research must answer and most important sub-questions).

1. Information missing on most important question and sub-questions derived from the research problem.
2. Summary of research problem (most important question) and most important sub-questions.
3. Satisfactory overview of most important question, sub-questions.
4. Logically organized overview of most important question, sub-questions, and aspired contribution to the discipline.
5. Logically organized and excellent communicated overview of most important question, sub-questions, and aspired contribution to the field.

8.3 In-session activities

Action

Before the session, the participants send the completed Question Practicum to one of their colleagues. To this end, you have formed duos of participants who will give each other feedback during the session. They each have 30 minutes to do so. Then the whole group comes together again.

> You make an inventory of the main results of this peer review. You then present your own key conclusions that you formulated while reading the participants' Question Practicums.
>
> You start your general recommendations in response to the submitted work. Then you can explain your most important conclusions and recommendations regarding the Question Practicum of each participant.

8.4 Post-session assignment

> **Action**
>
> In this assignment, students will formulate the central research question for their proposal, and the sub-questions, departing from a clear research problem and indicating the innovative character/relevance of their research and the way it is embedded in theory and the existing literature (the literature overview is taken as a benchmark). They will depart from the knowledge acquired in the sessions on 'embedding and relevance' and 'from topic to question'. They will send you this paper and discuss it with their (potential) supervisor.

9 Session 7: theory, hypothesis and claim

We have arrived at the part of the proposal that frightens many PhD candidates: THE THEORY. One of the explanations for this is the wide variety of views on what a theory is. Let us present some useful perspectives. For example, Pawson and Tilley (2008) who see theories as 'generative causal propositions'; Rosenthal (cited in Meltzoff, 2007: 28) makes the important distinction between various levels of theory:

> Theory is like a large-scale map, with the different areas representing general principles and the connections between them being sets of logical rules. Hypotheses ... are like small sectional maps, which focus only on specific areas ... Second, hypotheses (being more focused) are more directly amenable to empirical confrontation.

I will go deeper into the definition of a theory as a well-reasoned proposition or hypothesis. My suspicion is that most of the PhD research is focused on collecting and analysing primary and secondary data for which working hypotheses are especially useful. The distinction between various levels of theory ties in with authors who, for example, made a distinction between grand theories and theories of the middle range.

Bordens and Abbott (2008: 30) address the confusion that often exists in the scientific community regarding the term 'theory'. They start by distinguishing between a theory and a hypothesis. They point out how in the scientific writing 'theory', 'hypothesis', 'law' and 'model' are mixed up (ibid.: 31). They state:

> Theories are more complex than hypotheses. In contrast to the simple one-variable account provided by [a] hypothesis, a theory would account for changes ... by specifying the action and interaction of a system of variables ... no single observation could substantiate the theory in its entirety.

A second major distinction is that between theory as a starting point or as a goal. With the concept of 'grounded theory', Glaser and Strauss (2009) described the theory as a goal, as a result. In several disciplines, research is being done in previously unexplored areas. Broader theoretical perspectives or perspectives that could be used in related fields may be helpful, but the theory in that new field will be developed rather than evaluated.

9.1 Different perspectives on theory

Pawson and Tilley (2008: 120) make the lives of our PhD candidates easier by making it clear that there are many different perspectives regarding the definition and role of the theory. They distinguish, for example, theory in the sense of the following meanings:

- General orientations
- Ad hoc or ex post factum interpretations
- Empirical generalizations
- Derivations and codifications
- Axiomatic systems
- Hypotheses
- Explanations
- Paradigms
- Conceptual frameworks
- Causal propositions

You will advocate your own definition within your programme and explain which traditions are leading in your own work and that of your colleagues. It is important and reassuring for your students to know that there is not one sacred definition of the theory. The crucial point again is that you do not assume that your students already know what a theory is and what role it plays in their research. That is what this meeting is about.

9.2 Theory within a PhD research proposal: the propositions

In my own programme, I have always worked with the following working definition of theory:

> A theory is a collection of well-motivated, disciplinary embedded and researchable propositions/theses that try to explain or try to understand, for example, the existence or non-existence of a problem, the similarities, and differences between A&B, the (in)effectiveness of a measure, the plausibility of a development.

It is not my intention to focus on a specific interpretation of the term 'theory'. That is up to you and your research environment. It will help your students to address the difference between theory and hypothesis in this regard as well as the role of theory in research. Bordens and Abbott (2008) distinguish understanding, prediction, organizing and interpreting research results, generating research ('providing ideas for new research'). They then discuss the characteristics of a good theory and strategies for testing theories.

They conclude with the distinction between theory-driven versus data-driven research. This distinction comes close to the concept of 'grounded theory' that Glaser and Strauss launched in 1967 (revised in 2009): the discovery of theory from data systematically obtained from research. This approach can be especially useful where theories are not yet available for developing propositions. Where neither the 'grand theories' nor 'theories of the middle range' can assist in formulating specific claims regarding our subject that has not been researched before.

9.3 Ultimate focus in a proposal: formulation of the argument and claims

A must read for all your students is Booth et al. (2008: Part III, 'Making an argument'). We already met this book when it discussed 'From topic to question'. I summarize their main thoughts regarding the value of a claim in scientific research. In this chapter they discuss how to evaluate the clarity and significance of the claim that answers your students' research question.

> You need a tentative answer to your research question to focus your research for the data that will test and support its answer …The kind of problem you pose determines the kind of claim you make and the kind of argument you need to support it … Academic researchers usually pose not practical problems but conceptual ones, the kind whose solution asks readers not to act but to understand … Do not try to inflate the importance of a conceptual claim by taking on a practical action, at least not early in your report. If you want to suggest a practical application of your conceptual claim, do it in your conclusion. There you can offer it as an action worth considering without having to develop a case for it.
>
> (ibid., pp. 129, 122)

9.4 Script for the session

Preparatory reading

Before the session, you ask your students to search and read literature about the role of theory in the scientific research in their discipline. These texts can be ones that deal with the role of the theory in a general sense, or in a specific domain, or the role of the theory in a specific research project.

Your introduction

- Presentation of different definitions of theory
- Levels of theory: grand theories, theories of the middle range, specific topical theories
- Roles of theory, for example, understanding, predicting, organizing and interpreting research results
- Theory-driven research versus data-driven research
- Grounded theory
- Characteristics of a good theory

You also present the criteria that are involved when assessing the theoretical quality of a proposal (see also Appendix G, Section 2).

Relevant elements in the evaluation of theoretical quality

'Theoretical context' including research's position in the specialist field(s) (particularly in relation to other research), research theme(s) contained in the problem, choices and presuppositions concerning the subject matter, rationale for these choices and presuppositions, and definitions of the main concepts. Contribution to the disciplinary state of the art.

Rubric

1= Lack of theoretical context/Theory section *lacking* an arguable theoretical position in outline. Documentation is poorly constructed or absent. Aspired contribution to the discipline not mentioned.

2= Theory section clarifying in outline the theoretical context of the research, *needing greater care* in documenting sources, greater effort in organizing the text and/or a deeper level of analysis. Information on the aspired contribution to the discipline is not included.

3= Selective literature review *adequately clarifying some* of the relevant elements of the research context. Indications with respect to the possible contribution to the discipline.

4= Selective and critical literature review *effectively clarifying most of* the relevant elements of the research context, *formulating a tentative position with respect to the aspired contribution to the discipline.*

5= Selective and critical literature review, *effectively clarifying all* the relevant elements of the research context, *formulating a clear and robust position with respect to the aspired contribution to the discipline.*

> **Action**
>
> There are many different views on what a theory is. Present some of those that are doing the rounds within your discipline. Ask your participants to indicate the strengths and weaknesses in the different views on theory and their own preferred interpretation of the concept of theory.

Presentation by a colleague: the role of the theory in the research

It is instructive to have one of your colleagues or a PhD candidate illustrate the role of theory through his or her own research.

In-session activity

> **Action**
>
> - You split up the group in to couples interviewing each other on the aspect of theory in the proposal (15 minutes each).
> - The interviewer will zoom in on the type of theory, the role of the theory and the theoretical relevance in the proposal of the interviewee.
> - What does the theory mean for the proposal of the interviewee? Which role is the theory playing in terms of …
>   - understanding;
>   - prediction;
>   - organizing and interpreting research results?
> - The interviewer tries to receive an answer that is as specific as possible on what the proposed research intends to add to the state of the art of the knowledge in the field. The interviewee answers based on the results of the literature search up to now.
> - Afterwards, you will make a little round to ask the interviewers whether they felt the answers were clear (enough) for them and what they learned from their colleague's answers.

10 Session 8: the research design

In this session, you as a researcher and the methodologists and colleagues from your own discipline have the floor.

> Choosing an appropriate research design is crucially important to the success of your project. The decisions you make at this stage of the research process do much determine the quality of the conclusions that you can draw from your research results.
>
> (Bordens and Abbott, 2008: 97)

This session identifies the questions to be answered when choosing a research design and introduces different types of research design.

In view of the proposal, the central question is whether the students have clearly outlined their research design and research methods. The participants may already have research experience and have had introductions to the different design possibilities, methods, and techniques in your discipline. With the help of this session, they will apply any existing knowledge in their own research design. This session offers you the opportunity to determine whether their knowledge in the aforementioned areas is indeed available and where additional training outside your programme is necessary.

As in Chapter 3, I make suggestions for how this session can be structured. Again, you will make it your own. Input from scientists from the field of the participants in your Proposal Lab is essential.

> **Action**
>
> It is impossible to present books on research design in the various disciplines here. For this session, ask your participants to do an internet search for books written about research design in their discipline. They will be amazed at what is available. There may be a book among the results that you would like to read with the whole group.

10.1 What we may expect from the methods and data section in a proposal

My colleague Heinze Oost laid the foundation for the assessment of this part of the proposal.

Methods

Relevant elements are:

1 Function of the research (describing, comparing, defining, evaluating, explaining, designing)
2 Sample (segment of the population [universe of units or objects] that is selected for research, for example, locations, periods, objects, actors, etc.)
3 The properties or attributes of object(s) of research (to be compared, described, evaluated, etc.)
4 Data-collection methods

> **Rubric**
>
> 1= Lack of methods section/Methods section showing hardly any information on research function, sample, object properties and methods.
> 2= Methods section lacking relevant information on the research function, sample, object properties and methods. And/or level of analysis needs improvement.
> 3= Methods section adequately clarifying research function, sample, object properties and methods. Level of analysis is satisfactory but is lacking details in motivation.
> 4= Methods section effectively clarifying research function, sample, object properties and methods. Level of analysis and motivation are good.
> 5= Methods section effectively clarifying research function, sample, object properties and methods. Level of analysis and motivation are excellent.

10.2 Pre-session assignment

> **Action**
>
> As a preparation for the session, you ask your students to think about how they are going to answer the central research question (and sub-questions) of their research project. In other words, what data they will need to answer these questions, and what their research methods will be. They write this down on one A4 sheet, bring it to the session and send it to you a couple of days before the session.

> **Action**
>
> Critical appraisal of methods sections in the proposal of two predecessors. Some time before the session, send your students two proposals written by their predecessors. You ask the students to pay particular attention to the data and methods section in these proposals and to evaluate them against the criteria mentioned above. They bring their judgements to the session.
>
> Ask the participants to give their opinion in the form of advice: how could the colleagues have improved their research design?

10.3 Introduction by the teacher: some suggestions

Here are some building blocks for your own introduction. You design your own introduction in view of your own knowledge and scientific discipline. The main function of your introduction is to check whether your students are familiar with the core elements of the data and methods section in a proposal. Do they know what the expectations of their readers are? In addition, you and your students must determine whether the knowledge and skills are available to use specific methods of material collection.

Opening

We are approaching the real start of our project. There are some hurdles we must take before we can report our plans in the format of a Research Proposal.

- Yes, we have the questions, but which data do we need to answer our questions?
- We are working under limits of time and feasibility, so we must limit ourselves. We cannot study the whole world, all the cases, the total history, we can't interview all the possible informants … we must work on the selection of units (countries, cases, persons, documents, periods, experiments), in other words: the sample.
- Okay, we might have specified the data and the sample, but how then to collect our information, which methods of data collection and data analysis will we be using?

Why transparency?

Why is it important to offer our readers this information? We must comply with the important criteria in establishing and assessing the quality of our research. That starts with offering transparency on sampling and methods before we start the research (so that others can judge the quality of our approach and feasibility – ex ante evaluation) and after we have completed the project (so that others, for example, our supervisors, can evaluate the quality of our findings and report – ex post evaluation).

Where it all comes together is in creating transparency regarding how we will do it and how we have done it. Without transparency we cannot judge how a researcher has done something and we cannot judge why there is a good justification of doing it that way, if plausible alternatives have been overlooked, etc.

Basic elements of the data and methods section of a proposal

In each research project, the researcher selects methods to obtain the research findings. The researcher will be guided by prior knowledge or theories about the phenomena under study. The researcher's ideas might be intuitive or formulated as propositions or working hypotheses. In that way, the research process starts with a conceptual model of the object of research. That determines the questions that are to be answered and which procedures will be used to find answers to these questions. The research design shows the researcher's plan for collecting and organizing data and which specific rules and procedures will be followed.

Many alternatives are available regarding the nature of the research cases, the number of cases, the primary basis for selecting cases (sampling), basic sources of data, the methods of gathering the data, etc. Every decision should be well motivated in the proposal the candidates are preparing. After the primary research question has been defined, we will formulate a number of sub-questions whose answers allow us to answer the main question at the end of the research project. Sometimes we are inclined to formulate more questions than we need to answer the main question. This is a 'red flag' moment.

After we have formulated the sub-questions – and sometimes there is even a layer of sub-sub-questions – we will determine what kind of material we need to answer the questions and how we are going to collect this material. All these points must be clearly stated in our research proposal.

Corbin and Strauss (2008: 77, 247) suggest using comparison, process and context:

- Comparison
    - helps to obtain a grasp on the meaning of events that might otherwise seem obscure;
    - helps sensitize researchers to properties and dimensions that are in the data but remain obscure due to a lack of sensitivity on the part of the researcher;
    - counters the tendency to focus on a particular case;
    - forces researchers to examine their own basic assumptions, perspectives.
- Process – analysing data for process encourages the incorporation of variation into the findings; process can lead to the identification of patterns and trends.
- Context – identifies the sets of conditions in which problems and/or situations and/or arrangements or problems arise.

10.4 In-session assignments

Action

Evaluating the methods section in the proposals by predecessors. 'You have evaluated the method sections of two predecessors. Discuss your findings in three sub-groups. Report on the major strengths and weaknesses.'

Action

After the students' report, you will give your own comments on the work of the predecessors. You will be able to compare your observations with those of your students. Do this by formulating statements for discussion.

> You can refer to the research design and methods experts in your own discipline and criteria such as:
>
> 1. How defensible is the research design?
> 2. How well defended is the sample design/target selection of cases/documents?
> 3. Sample composition/case inclusion – how well is the eventual coverage described?
> 4. Contexts of data sources – how well are they retained and portrayed?
> 5. How well has diversity of perspective been explored?
> 6. How well are detail, depth and complexity (richness) of data been considered in the research design?

10.5 In-session assignment: explaining research questions and data collection to a peer

> **Action**
>
> The students bring to the session their plans regarding questions, data and methods (see the pre-session assignment).
> The students are placed in pairs and each student gets 15 minutes to tell their colleague:
>
> - what the central research question is;
> - what the sub-research questions are;
> - which (methodological) steps they will take to answer these questions.
>
> After these pairwise discussions, your group comes together again. Each student is asked to briefly explain the research of the interlocutor:
>
> - What is the central research question?
> - What kind of question is this?
> - How will the interlocutor answer these questions?
>
> Then the students are asked to give their opinion on the methodological steps that the interlocutor wishes to take.
> Finally, the interlocutor is asked to explain what has been learned: what he/she has learned:
>
> - from the exercise to explain the research in a simple way;
> - from the explanation and comments given by the colleague.

10.6 Closure of this session

After Session 8, all the components of the proposal are well explained. The participants will now start working on their Proposal Halfway. It is good to come back to the planning they have made for the development of their proposal at the end of this session. Are they still on track or are adjustments needed? Discuss with them the possibilities of giving each other peer support and in any case show that you are willing to have email contact or to meet in case they get stuck somewhere. And better before they reach that moment!

11 The third individual feedback meeting: the Proposal Halfway

11.1 The assignment

At this point, your participants have received sufficient information about the format of a proposal and the quality criteria that will be in force. You explained to them that writing a proposal is a growth process. That is why the programme first asks for a Proposal Halfway. They will discuss this with each other, experts, potential supervisors and you. On this basis, they will work for a few more weeks before submitting the Final Proposal.

11.2 The feedback

In this third individual feedback meeting, you will give feedback on the details of the Proposal Halfway. Preferably, you do this by writing down your comments. The students can compare the comments of the different feedback providers. At least where these overlap, there is serious work to be done.

It is an interesting option to have each participant attend a colleague's Proposal Halfway discussion with his/her supervisor. They take notes and discuss them afterwards with their colleague.

11.3 On the way to the final proposal

After this feedback, the students will continue to work on their Final Proposal for several weeks. This is the final part of their programme.

11.4 Interim contact and intervision meeting

Offer e-coaching or meeting each other if they run into questions or problems during the weeks they are working on their Final Proposal. A good option is to organize a meeting where your participants can present to their colleagues a problem they are struggling with while writing their proposal. The format is that of an intervision meeting with the difference that all participants have their turn. Form groups of a maximum of four participants who work according to the principles as explained in Chapter 3, Section 4.9, intervision.

5 What we will know after completion of the Proposal Lab

> **Reading tip**
>
> This chapter informs supervisors, Proposal Lab conveners and students about the results of the Proposal Lab and the qualities needed for a successful PhD project.

1 Different types of proposal writers

Let us start by sketching different types of potential PhD candidates. All of them passed a strict selection procedure; we had high expectations of them all, and we rated them among the top of their cohort. After 7–8 months, we can distinguish in a group of 18 talented students the following types:

- *The Certain Winners*: the students who 'have it', the students who bend assignments to their will and surprised us repeatedly – the candidates for a PhD project.
- *The Conditional Candidates:*
  - Passive Talents – certainly, the student is talented, but is passive, waits for our instructions repeatedly.
  - The Talented Topic Hopper – just when this talent has chosen a nice topic, the candidate enters our office announcing the project will be completely different.
  - Talented Rule Breaker – the talented student who does not stick to the rules of the game, who ignores deadlines, who fights a delayed battle of independence, creating much irritation with surrounding supervisors and lecturers.
- *The Fragile Talent* – the talented one who is feeling very uncertain, constantly needing our reassurance.

- Finally, *The (Provisional?) Non-Candidates*
    - Feeble Minimalist – the candidate who is cutting corners.
    - Talented Disappointers – actually, the most remarkable category, the students who have been selected without any doubt, but start to disappoint us during the programme. Two reasons why were dominant: combining study work with private activities that take up too much time or combining the main study with other study interests. In short, not giving enough time to the development of a PhD proposal. Or the other category, the student who is not feeling good, is having rough times privately and is dropping out now and then.

We came to this typology during an extended period of co-operation. We did not see the weaknesses during the admission procedure. These experiences illustrate the big problems we are confronted with in deciding on the admission of PhD candidates in our department. It is impossible to get a nuanced picture of qualities and risks during a procedure based on an examination of some written material, mostly insipid references, and a meeting of, let us say, 45 minutes. It confirms the value of a longer introductory period in the form of the Proposal Lab.

2 Predicting underperforming in proposal writing: is it possible?

Let us start with two anecdotes. Julia took part in our programme and was repeatedly overwhelmed with great doubts, scepticism in the immediate family circle and grief. Tears were shed every time we met. Everything in me told me that she was too fragile to complete a long-term PhD programme. While we knew that our meetings would always lead to a few tears, we could even laugh about that. 'Wait, Julia, I'll grab a box of tissues' … and then we would have fun and get to work constructively. Seven years later she successfully defended her PhD thesis.

There was also Louise. An extremely talented participant in our programme. We said to each other: 'a born PhD candidate!'. She was working hard, and then suddenly there were hiccups. Work was turned in hastily and below her level, and she did not seem quite there with her attention. We had to discuss a paper once; I suggested a day, but then Louise could not be there, telling that she had to be in [another university city]. Interested, I said, 'What are you going to do there?' A little shyly, she said that in addition to our programme, she had also started a Master's programme in a completely different discipline. I raised my eyebrows. She completed our programme with a good thesis plan, while I had the feeling that the fragmented attention would lead to nothing. A few years later, I saw that Louise had become one of the influential Dutch PhD representatives, had two children by now and was on her way to completing her thesis.

In the following I will outline several characteristics of PhD candidates of whom we can doubt whether a PhD trajectory is really something for them. Can we predict underperforming? What should we pay attention to?

The two anecdotes teach us that our observations during our programme may contain important clues as to the strengths and weaknesses of a candidate, but that it is possible that the candidates whom we doubted the most will produce a PhD thesis. So, do not let what follows lead to final judgements about suitability or not, but serve as important points of attention for the conversations we will have in our programme about their prospects of success. Having the following points in mind, we will make our students feel that we understand where they may have their shoes pinched. This is how we get further.

2.1 Substantive indicators for underperformance

1. The research topic 'shrinks' on closer study of the literature and the candidate cannot respond smoothly by changing course. There remains a small topic, of which the assessor wonders whether this requires 4 years of doctoral research.
2. The writer explicitly reports confusion on their side, in combination with procrastination.
3. Insufficient deep familiarity with the topic has arisen. The writer does not indicate that he or she has delved deep into the material. Insufficient exploration has taken place. The reader feels that the writer relies mainly on secondary sources and has not seen any primary material.
4. There is an unclear structuring of the argument in written texts. A characteristic of this is that the writer does not use headings and sub-headings. The reader must struggle through the text.
5. In written texts, a lack of structure takes the form of questions scattered throughout the text. The writer does not clearly put them together in summary or separate section, so that the reader can quickly assess the interrelationship between the questions.
6. The writer does not establish a link with the scientific exchange of views on their subject. The writer is not in conversation with colleagues, for example, via a strong literature review.
7. Some of our candidates show a familiarity with the literature but are not yet able to achieve a synthesis. The literature is presented as loose fragments without clarifying where the authors correspond or are in discussion. Another characteristic is the presentation of the literature per author and not thematically.
8. The writer does not provide a clear picture of the material needed to answer the research questions and the way in which he or she will collect them.
9. The writer assumes or claims that there are scientific problems but does not substantiate this statement or formulates no intention to investigate whether these problems exist and of which disciplinary nature they are.
10. Unsubstantiated claims are presented regarding the originality of the subject ('not yet researched', 'no other authors have written about it') or the possible causes of the assumed problem.

2.2 Behavioural indicators of underperformance

Manathunga (2005) mentioned as the most important warning signs as regards underperforming PhD candidates: frequent change of subject and frequent change of planning. In addition, she mentions isolating themselves from fellow doctoral candidates, department, or research institute, postponing submission of work and, in the first place, avoiding communication with the teachers or supervisors.

In my own practice I also found the following:

- Unforeseen change of subject. However, it should be noted that subject changes can also be enforced by external circumstances. A subject may unexpectedly turn out to be in the hands of another researcher. On the other hand, a wonderful new subject can also be thrown into one's lap, an opportunity not to be missed.
- Exceeding deadlines, especially if this is in combination with ...
- Non-communication with supervisors, lab conveners, etc.
- The authors present the lecturers with a *fait accompli* by failing to meet the deadlines and not informing them in time. Work to be handed in just comes in too late.
- Procrastination, 'there is always something the matter'.

2.3 Core themes in a lack of progress

1. Lack of progress: Few differences between different versions of texts, for example, drafts of the proposal.
2. Narrow-mindedness: Inadequate literature study and insufficient exploration of the field of study refer to a closed working attitude. The writer is not open to the work of others. Poor communication with you and potential supervisors can also be a characteristic of a closed working posture. It should be noted that an uninterested supervisor can also have a share in this!
3. Bias: The writer assumes a problem that needs a scientific answer (but does not investigate the actual existence of the problem) or assumes that the problem is of a specific disciplinary nature. The writers do not test their assumptions.
4. Wish for allies instead of critical appraisal: The student identifies with a specific position in the scientific discussion or a particular author and shows a lack of critical ability.
5. Instrumentalism and solutionism are dominant: Narrow-mindedness also arises from a strong fixation on the desire to create practical solutions (design lust). It can be a shocking experience for teachers to see how their students not only stagnate in their thinking about a research proposal, but even can deteriorate. In fundamental research, research Master's students and PhD candidates are challenged to ask fundamental questions, driven by

a theoretical ambition for explanation. At least, that was the message we conveyed to our students. One of our students has not been moving away from an instrumental perspective in her research but succeeded in doing the opposite: solutionism and design lust did become more prominent at the expense of more fundamental questions that she presented earlier.

2.4 The candidates' evaluations

One participant rated the programme as follows:

> It was very good that in this programme, you had the opportunity to make the assignments in line with your own research proposal. Therefore, this course really helped me in writing and doing research for my own research proposal ... I liked the 'free thinking' that was possible during the programme. A great deal of the programme involved one's own research and not plainly reading materials, as happens in other courses. It really distinguished itself as a course ... I'm glad to have an insight into other research methods as well. It makes you more aware of the strengths and weaknesses of [specific kinds of] research. I also liked the time for discussions in class and in general the assignments were very helpful to proceed in your research/topic choice.

Aspects mentioned by the participants in an appreciative sense: the practical assignments, the feedback from the convener, topics discussed and their order, useful skills training, the pressure on the participants to advance in their research and to work on the proposal, the coaching/mentoring approach, getting to know about the research projects of others and the freedom concerning the student's topics.

In critical observations, participants emphasized the importance of the clarity of assignments, putting more effort in explaining what is expected from participants, the balance between conveners when it comes to team teaching, and staying involved as a convener and keeping contact in the period when the participants work more individually on their proposal. It is also important to plan the programme in such a way that the timing of the completion of the proposal corresponds to the submission dates that apply in an admission procedure for a PhD position. The proposal deadlines ought to be synchronized with the deadline for a PhD application.

One of the evaluators emphasized the tension that can arise between the Proposal Lab convener, and, on the other hand, the supervisor, being much more positive or negative.

2.5 Final chord

Does the quality of the proposal lead to a final assessment of the qualities of students and early PhD candidates? Years ago, I made an overview of the proposal assessments of the PhD candidates of my graduate school, at the end

Table 5.1 Report on a PhD student's work

Evaluator	Appreciation	Criticism
Evaluator 1		Paper makes a very unfinished impression; why are the experiences of [migrants] interesting; central problem is unclear. Which theoretical framework? Can get stranded in the mess of data. Provisional chapter layout reflects book's fragile structure.
Evaluator 2	Little to criticize about empirical research, careful approach, a lot of material	Meagre theorizing; danger of a highly descriptive study
Evaluator 3	Convincing piece of work. Follow her progress with respect.	
Evaluator 4	Undoubtedly has interesting material and gives it fascinating elaboration	She is bad at expressing herself simply and clearly. What exactly she has in her hands and which questions she wants to impose on material remain unclear. Apparently, she works by touch. Extension of planned timetable is a major concern. Clarification and specification of research plans are necessary (= discussion of work plan).

of their first year of the PhD programme. There was a lot of criticism. The evaluators – full professors from the graduate school and colleagues of the supervisors – complained about a lack of grip on the literature, methodological weaknesses, unclear formulation of the problem, a lack of limitation in the research ambitions, a missing leading argument and, above all, theoretical infirmities. What is striking is the combination of criticism and appreciation. I give you an illustration, the comments on the work of candidate 'E' (Table 5.1).

A couple of years later, 'E' defended her doctoral thesis and became a highly regarded independent researcher.

Twenty years after these often-critical assessments of proposals and research plans, we know in many cases how the careers of these 23 PhD candidates developed. Seven were appointed to full professors and six became senior lecturers. There are three independent, highly respected, scientific researchers and one became a publisher.

We know for sure that one has not yet defended his thesis. In five cases, it is unknown what have been the next steps in their career after their time at the graduate school. What we can learn from this is that assessing a proposal is part of a formative assessment. We get feedback on the progress and clues on what needs to be done. In exceptional cases, the proposal provides material for a final assessment of the qualities of the students and early PhD candidates.

The biggest benefit of a Proposal Lab is that after completing the proposal, students and supervisors know exactly what they are getting into if both parties decide on a multi-year PhD trajectory and intensive collaboration.

Appendices
Tools for students, PhD candidates and supervisors

A. The writing of a proposal and being a PhD candidate: Literature tips for teachers, supervisors, students and PhD candidates
B. Example of a Proposal Lab prospectus
C. Example of a Proposal Lab schedule (September–June)
D. The Snapshot: Students' information about research interests
E. The Rough Topic Exploration: In-class assignment, Session 1
F. Planning the well-reasoned topic choice and proposal design: In-class assignment, Session 2
G. Proposal information and tips: Session 3
   Writing the proposal abstract
   Rubrics for evaluating the proposal qualities
   Criteria for evaluating research questions
H. A well-reasoned topic choice: Guidelines for students and PhD candidates
I. Instructions in form format for writing the Proposal Halfway
J. The disciplinary embedding assignment, Session 4 and Session 5
K. The Question Practicum: Session 6
L. Evaluating individual research training assignments
   Evaluation of interview reports
   Evaluation of the literature search report
   Evaluation of the critical appraisals
   Evaluation of a literature review
M. SWOT Analysis by candidates already halfway to a proposal (the Clinic)
N. Expectations in view of a 4 year PhD project
O. Planning Matrix PhD trajectory: Research and other activities
P. At the end of the proposal journey: SWOT analysis in view of a (future) PhD project
Q. Training and supervision plan

Appendix A
The writing of a proposal and being a PhD candidate
Literature tips for teachers, supervisors, students and PhD candidates

Note: The books I present here sometimes have their origins in a specific disciplinary field and have been of great value to the Proposal Lab. The reason I mention them lies also in the fact that they have a value far beyond the limits of that specific discipline.

Aveyard, H. (2007) *Doing a Literature Review in Health and Social Care: A Practical Guide.* Maidenhead: Open University Press.

This book covers all the important aspects of doing a literature review: why do a literature review, what literature will be relevant, developing a research question, how to search for literature and how to critically appraise it, how to present my review.

Greenhalgh, T. (2010): *How to Read a Paper: The Basics of Evidence-Based Medicine.* Oxford: Wiley-Blackwell.

Written for researchers in evidence-based medicine, it triggers the critical appraisal of literature in many other disciplines.

Phillips, E.M. and Johnson, C.G. (2022) *How to Get a PhD: A Handbook for Students and Their Supervisors* (7th edn). Maidenhead: Open University Press.

Especially:

- Chapter 4, 'How not to get a PhD'
- Chapter 7, 'The PhD process'
- Chapter 11, 'How to supervise and examine' (among others: what students expect of their supervisors)

Booth, W.C., Colomb, G.G., Williams. J.M., Bizup, J. and FitzGerald, W.T. (2016) *The Craft of Research* (4th edn). Chicago: The University of Chicago Press.

- Chapter 3, 'From topics to questions'
- Chapter 4, 'From questions to a problem'

- Chapter 5, 'From problems to sources'
- Chapter 6, 'Engaging sources'
- Chapter 7, 'Making good arguments'
- Chapter 8, 'Making claims'

Lovitts, B.E. (2007) *Making the Implicit Explicit: Creating Performance Expectations for the Thesis.* Sterling, VA: Stylus Publishing.

This is a book that every PhD candidate should read. It makes clear on which criteria a dissertation will be judged. It specifies the criteria for 10 different disciplines. These are easily applicable to other related disciplines.

Verschuren, P. and Doorewaard, H. (2005) *Designing a Research Project.* Utrecht: Lemma.

Brewer, R. (2007) *Your PhD Thesis: How to Plan, Draft, Revise and Edit Your Thesis.* Abergele: Studymates Limited.

- Chapter 2, 'Different types of research'
- Chapter 3, 'The research question'
- Chapter 4, 'Feasibility'
- Chapter 5, 'The research proposal'

Gosling, P. and Noordam, B. (2006) *Mastering Your PhD: Survival and Success in the Doctoral Years and Beyond.* Berlin: Springer-Verlag.

- Chapter 2, 'Getting started'
- Chapter 3, 'Setting goals and objectives'
- Chapter 8, 'The art of good communication'
- Chapter 10, 'Searching the scientific literature'

Becker, H.S. (1986) *Writing for Social Scientists: How To Start And Finish Your Thesis, Book, Or Article.* Chicago: University of Chicago Press.

Becker, H.S. (1998) *Tricks of the Trade: How to Think About Your Research While You're Doing It.* Chicago: The University of Chicago Press.

Meltzoff, J. (2007) *Critical Thinking About Research: Psychology and Related Fields* (9th edn). Washington, DC: American Psychological Association.

- Chapter 1, 'Critical reading'
- Chapter 2, 'Research questions and hypotheses'

Hunt, J. and Nhlengethwa, S. (2009) *The Art of the Idea and How It Can Change Your Life.* New York: PowerHouse Books.

- Observation No. 03, 'Ideas have moods'
- Observation No. 06. 'I google therefore I am (not)'
- Observation No. 07, 'Trust your instincts or they will go away'
- Observation No. 08, 'Incremental change is fine if you are a glacier'

Delamont, S., Atkinson, P. and Parry, O. (2004) *Supervising the Doctorate: A Guide to Success*. London: The Society for Research into Higher Education.

- Chapter 2, 'Caught and held by a cobweb: getting the student started'
- Chapter 3, 'The balance between tradition and progress: designing and planning a project'
- Chapter 4, 'Old manuscripts: the literature review'
- Chapter 5, 'Heavy and thankless task: overseeing the data collection'
- Chapter 11, 'A rather unpromising consignment: selecting successful students and building a research culture'

Okorocha, E. (2007) *Supervising International Research Students*. London: Society for Research into Higher Education.

Snieder, R. and Larner, K. (2009) *The Art of Being a Scientist: A Guide for Graduate Students and Their Mentors*. Cambridge: Cambridge University Press.

- Chapter 2, 'What is science?'
- Chapter 3, 'Choices, choices, choices'
- Chapter 5, 'Questions drive research'
- Chapter 6, 'Giving direction to our work'
- Chapter 8, 'Ethics of research'

> Realize that there are countless resources on the internet that provide comparable information. You can also use the literature description above to develop search terms that will help you to locate possible internet sources. But in any given case, make sure that you carefully search the internet or alternative literature for the topics covered in the above literature descriptions.

Appendix B
Example of a Proposal Lab prospectus

Title of the programme: The writing of a PhD proposal
Lecturers: _____

Prerequisites: Being registered as Research MA/Master's student/PhD candidate/MPhil candidate. Willingness to read, discuss, write and rewrite with enthusiasm, perseverance and an open mind for everything that seems new.

1 Overview of Proposal Lab objectives

The Proposal Lab will deal with:

- the development of a solid research design;
- individual research skills;
- the formulation of a research proposal;
- an introduction to research strategies and methods of data collection (in that way functioning as an entry point to the detailed study of specific methods);
- learning how to manage yourself and your supervisor;
- learning to critically reflect on your own writings and assess the scientific quality of scholarly publications.

The Proposal Lab is designed to provide students with faculty guidance and peer support in undertaking the writing of an elaborated research proposal as a stand-alone exercise or as the basic material for an application for a PhD position or a research position of shorter duration in or outside academia. Parallel to the Proposal Lab, students will have to foster an intensive co-operation with their 'faculty mentors'. The Proposal Lab is not intended as a substitute for specialized training on particular topics, which the participants may expect from teachers in domain courses, mentors and/or supervisors.

Besides the proposal development, the Proposal Lab contains a section that will provide students with an introduction 'light' in individual research skills and [specific disciplinary] research methods.

2 Lab objectives in detail

We distinguish three major building blocks: knowledge, skills and application. In the overview that follows, you will find the specificities per building block.

A. Objective 1. Knowledge of
- newest developments in the discipline
- the function of theory in research
- the function of the research question and the different types of research questions
- the components of a research proposal and the elements of a research design
- the criteria that are used in the evaluation of research designs and research proposals.

B. Objective 2. Skills
- basic ingredients of intellectual craftmanship
- interviewing experts
- searching the most important literature
- critical appraisal of literature
- writing a literature review
- finding a research niche for starting a new project
- extrapolation: reflection on one's own research interests and research experiences for making new research driven choices
- assembling research questions, formulation of data needed to answer the question and methods to collect the necessary data
- reporting and communication with respect one's own research
- giving and handling feedback (by Lab conveners, mentors/supervisors, and peers)
- complying with deadlines.

C. Objective 3. Application and synthesis
- application of knowledge and skills in the development of one's own research plans
- synthesis by putting together knowledge and skills in the development of a research proposal.

3 Lab requirements

Grades for the Lab will be based on participant's performances on the assignments during and concluding the sessions as well as the final proposal.

Preparatory reading

Students will prepare every session by studying the related literature. In that way, emphasis is put on discussing important aspects and exemplars, next to practising.

Assignments

During the Lab we will work with special assignments that contribute to the final product/outcome of the programme, namely: a full-size research proposal according to the format of a national research foundation. This consists of an abstract, a research problem (leading question and sub-questions), a methods paragraph, and a section on scientific and societal relevance. Sometimes we will hand out assignments that will serve as 'homework'.

The assignments provide opportunities for you to further develop and articulate your thinking about research design and research proposals. We expect the assignments to be prepared with due care and precision. A lack of cooperation will be reflected in the grading.

Turning assignments in

'Pre-assignments' will be done and turned in during the sessions.

The format of all the documents will be that of a Word document. Assignments that serve as homework will be sent to the students via electronic mail at least 7 days before the following Lab session. During this session, the results of the assignment will be discussed, among others by showing 'good practices' on the part of the students.

There will be three Individual Feedback Meetings.

1 The first will be devoted to discussing the Snapshot and the Rough Topic Exploration Matrix.
2 In the second meeting, we will discuss your well-reasoned topic choice.
3 The third one will be devoted to discussing the Proposal Halfway.

The deadline for the major assignments is (as an example):

- After 3 months: A well-reasoned topic choice.
- After 7–8 months: Proposal Halfway.
- After 9½ months: The Proposal Final Version.

Exemplars

One aim of the Proposal Lab is to promote exposure to the diversity of research and research proposals. This goal will be pursued by studying thesis summaries and research proposals by researchers in your domain, as well as by introductions by experienced researchers. 'Peer review' will also play an important role: you will read and evaluate the work of your fellow students.

Attendance

If you are not going to be able to attend, teachers expect to be informed by email about the reasons for not attending.

Books to be bought

[To be specified]

Overview of assignments to be graded

Table 6.1 Overview of Proposal Lab assignments to be graded

	Assignment	Deadline
a	Literature Review	
b	Research Question and Embedding Report	
c	Literature Search Report	
d	Interview Report	
e	Proposal Halfway	
f	Final Proposal	

Explanation of the intermediate assignments

1 A well-reasoned topic choice. After about 2½ months, you will complete your 'topic exploration'. You will write a paper entitled 'A well-reasoned topic choice'. This paper has the following required components:

  1 An Introduction containing information on the following points
     - The importance for the author of the topic exploration
     - The way in which the author has come to the choice of topics which have been researched in detail
     - The global approach of the topic exploration
     - The sources that were used for further exploration of the topics
     - A preview of the composition or structure of the text that will follow (roadmap for the reader).
  2 The approach of the 'topic exploration' and your evaluation of the approach: what went well?, where did you meet problems?, how did you solve them?
  3 What do five obvious 'sources of inspiration' tell you about the possible topics?
     a Your own previous study and research activities
     b Experts, possible supervisors, peers, etc.
     c The literature
     d Studied case material and examples, your own social experiences
     e Your personal 'research file' (see Wright Mills (1970), 'On intellectual craftmanship').
  4 A comparative strength/weakness analysis of the various topics that you have examined and considered.

Which topic will you choose after careful consideration? This choice reflects your ideas and thinking after 2½ months. In the months that follow, your ideas will change. That is a natural thing. Provide the following information:

1. The function of the topic and subsequent proposal: to be developed in view of a Master's thesis, or PhD proposal, or application for internal or external PhD position, or to be written as a 'stand-alone' exercise in writing a proposal.
2. Location of possible execution of the research to be prepared by writing the proposal.
3. Supervision/mentorship: who can supervise and advise you in the process of proposal writing?
4. Issues that are still open, points which one wishes to want to discuss with the Proposal Lab convenor(s).

The paper contains a bibliography of 20 texts (articles, book chapters, books) you consider to be closely related to your topic. These texts should be written by other researchers.

Size of the paper: Introduction: a maximum of half a page
Body: 2500 (min.) to 3000 words (max.)
Bibliography of 20 texts.

4 Extract of a literature review, based on at least five texts

Consult Appendix L, Section 4 for a suggested structure of this literature review. This Appendix can be added to the Proposal Lab prospectus.

A good literature review shows a critical appraisal of the literature. This means students will assess the articles and books from a peer review perspective. They will indicate the strong and weak aspects of the work in question in terms of quality and methodology, the type of research that is used, whether there is a sharp problem formulation and a clear research question, whether the research question is answered. For this aspect of the review, you will depart from the knowledge acquired in the session on 'writing a critical appraisal'. Take the 'Evaluation of the critical appraisals' form in Appendix L, Section 3 as a checklist while writing your critical appraisal.

5 Research question and embedding report

In this assignment, students will write down the research question for their planned research proposal, departing from a clear research problem and indicating the innovative character/relevance of their research and the way it is embedded in theory and the existing literature (the literature search and review are taken as your benchmark). In writing this note, you will depart from the knowledge acquired in the sessions on 'Embedding and relevance' and 'From topic to question'. This note is laying the foundation for your Proposal Halfway.

6 Interview report

You will write a report on two of your interviews. Components of the report:

- The two interview guides (maximum 2 pages in total).
- Two brief reports on the substance (the major results) of the interviews (maximum 2 x 3 pages). See also Appendix L, Section 1, Evaluation of interview reports.

7 Literature search report

Generic format for literature search report

1. Introduction:
    - Introduction of major research questions that have guided the search process
2. Preparation of the literature search:
    - Keywords, search terms and synonyms
    - Databases
    - Deciding on inclusion and exclusion criteria
    - Inclusion criteria
    - Exclusion criteria
3. The literature search in action:
    - Electronic databases
    - Reference list searching ('snowballing')
    - Talking to experts
4. Judging relevance of publications.
5. The way the results of the literature search are stored.
6. Strengths and limitations of the way the search process has been performed.
7. A short conclusion (which major problems have been found, how they have been solved, lessons for future search actions).
    - Annex 1: keywords, search terms
    - Annex 2: key references (20 most important documents that have been found by the literature search).

8 Evaluation criteria for Proposal Halfway and Final Proposal

The rubrics for the assessment of the Proposal Halfway and the final result, the Proposal, can be found in Appendix G, Section 2. This information can be added as an appendix to the Proposal Lab prospectus.

Appendix C

Example of Proposal Lab schedule (September–June)

Table 6.2 On the way to a (PhD) research proposal: a possible scheme

Topic	Moment	Didactics	Assignment	Texts
Pre-orientation on possible topics by participants by filling in Snapshot	Before start of Lab		Sent to teachers before start of programme by email attachment, August	
a. Introduction round convener and participants	Session 1, third week of September	Opening by convener(s)		
b. Preparing Research	Session 1	Introduction by convener(s)		
The Topic Exploration	Session 1	Instruction by convener(s)	In-class assignments: The Rough Topic Exploration Form	Appendix E
The Bigger Picture: • Research design • Research Proposal	Session 1	Instruction • Presentation of proposal format and two strong proposals. • Introduction of the literature	In class: Planning topic exploration Skimming some proposals Finger exercise in formulating topic + conceptual problem	Appendix F

(Continued)

Table 6.2 (Continued)

Topic	Moment	Didactics	Assignment	Texts
Individual feedback on Snapshot + Rough Topic Exploration	First week of October	Lab convener(s)	Snapshot and Rough Topic Exploration, handed in ultimately end of September	
Introduction on different types of research in the discipline [X]: the tricks of the trade	Session 2, Third week of October, Part I	Introduction on different types of research in discipline [X]. Researchers will first give some theoretical insights. Second, they will give examples of research that they have conducted themselves and will discuss with the students to which 'type' of research in discipline [X] this research would belong.		
Interviewing experts and informants with practical experiences	Part II	Interview instruction: Lab convener Comment on interview questions as prepared by participants during this session.	• Pre-session assignment: preparing interview questions for interviewing peer + draft of email for interview with expert and supervisors • Interview practicum • Post-session: interviewing two experts and writing of interview report	1 Bryman (2008) 2 'Semi-structured interview' 3 Appendix L, Section 1
Preparing contacting possible mentors/ supervisors	Part III	Instruction by Lab convener		

(Continued)

Table 6.2 (Continued)

Topic	Moment	Didactics	Assignment	Texts
Planning the proposal development	Part IV	Instruction by Lab convener	In-session: participants write down their own planning	Appendix F
Introduction of proposal format	Session 3, first week of November	• Explaining format • Presentation of evaluation criteria • Discussion of good practices	In sub-groups, the students discuss the qualities of two proposals they have been sent before the session After the session, students write a reflection paper on the implications of the literature study, convener's introductions and proposals they have read	1 Brewer (2007), Chapter 5 2 Good example by predecessor 3 Appendices G and I
Training in literature search	Session 4, third week of November, Part I	Introduction and practicum by librarians	Pre-session assignment: Students send note on research topic and research questions to librarians Instruction + In-class practicum Post-session: literature search and writing literature search report	1 Aveyard (2007), Chapters 1–4 2 Appendix L, Section 2

(Continued)

Appendix C **157**

Table 6.2 (Continued)

Topic	Moment	Didactics	Assignment	Texts
Embedding and relevance	Session 4, Part II	Introduction by Lab convener	1 Embedding assignment, in class 2 Discussing two thesis summaries.	1 Booth (2016), 'Engaging sources' 2 Appendix J
Writing a literature review	Session 5, second week of December, Part I	Sub-group discussion and evaluation of a literature review in the discipline [X]. Instruction by Lab convener	Pre-session reading of good practices in Literature Review. Post-session assignment: Students will write a literature review in view of their research topic. They will depart from the knowledge acquired in this session on 'writing a literature review'.	1 Aveyard (2007), Chapter 8 2 Evaluation scheme for literature review Appendix L, Section 4
Note-taking and critically appraising reports and documents	Session 5, Part II	Introduction by Lab convener Introduction of literature on criteria which can be used to assess (the quality of) research in the discipline [X]	1 Discussion of critical appraisal criteria in class 2 Post-session assignment: students will assess a substantial article in the discipline [X] from a peer review perspective.	1 Aveyard (2007), 'Critical reading' 2 Appendix L, Section 3
Second individual feedback meeting	Third week of December	Discussion of 'A well-reasoned topic choice' with Lab convener	Paper 'A well-reasoned topic choice'.	

(Continued)

Table 6.2 (Continued)

Topic	Moment	Didactics	Assignment	Texts
Questioning your topic	Session 6, second week of January	*From topic to question.* Introduction by Lab convener	In-session assignment: The Question Practicum. Post-session: students formulate the central research question for their proposal, and the sub-questions	1 Booth (2016), Chapter 3, 'From topic to questions' 2 Appendix K
Handing in: • Literature review • Critical appraisal Research question and embedding report	Second week of January			See Appendix for details of quality criteria
Theory, hypothesis, claim	Fourth week of January	Introduction by Lab convener: different perspectives on theory, the role of propositions and claim, and criteria that are involved when assessing the theoretical quality of a proposal One of the convener's colleagues or a PhD candidate illustrates the role of the theory within his or her own research	Lab participants split up in couples, interviewing each other on the aspect of theory in the proposal	Literature on theory in the specific discipline [x]
The research design: data and methods	Session 7, second week of February	Introduction by Lab convener and presentations by researchers, providing 'showcases' of research		Literature on the research design in the specific discipline [x]

(Continued)

Appendix C **159**

Table 6.2 (Continued)

Topic	Moment	Didactics	Assignment	Texts
Handing in: • Report on literature search • Interview report	March 1			Appendix L
Presenting your research ideas in progress	Session 8, first week of March	Students will prepare a 15-minute presentation of their research plans in progress. Each will be followed by a 15-minutes evaluation by peers and lecturers		Think of literature on presenting work in progress
Handing in Proposal Halfway	1 May			
Third individual feedback meeting: Proposal Halfway	To be decided			
Handing in Proposal Final Version	15 June			
Grading of Final Proposal	22 June			

Appendix D
The Snapshot
Students' information about research interests

Research interest and topic(s) under consideration (max. 1000 words in total)

Name:_____

Please answer the following questions clearly and in 'simple words'. Write for an academic, but non-specialist reader. See how much you can say. If you do not know the answer, leave the answer space empty. Feel free to give information about research experiences outside the field of research outside the discipline of your study. You may incorporate information you wrote down in the motivation letter.

History

1 The origin of your interest in general in doing research

Why are you interested in doing research [in the discipline of your study]? Where and when did your interest develop itself?

2 Prior research experiences

Have you been involved in research before? What was the major question? What was the major result, the major answer? [Answer this question also in case of research experiences you consider as limited or modest or outside your current field of interest.]

3 Your research capital

In your prior research experience, which of your personal and intellectual qualities were to your entire satisfaction? Where did you encounter the greatest problems?

4 What was the central question you have tried to answer in your most important prior research project?

On the way to a new research project

1 What is your research about?

Say something about the topic(s) you have in mind.

2 How much is already known about your topic(s)?

Can you explain in a few words what is known and what is still unknown with respect to your topic(s)?

3 Why is this research interesting for you?

4 Interesting for others?

Your research will be interesting for other people too. Please mention them and explain why they will be interested in your research and its results.

5 Discussion with others?

Have you already discussed you research interests and topics with others? What were their questions and suggestions?

6 Is your research connected to your disciplinary field?

In which way is your research topic connected with your prior disciplinary training?

You will participate in a [……..] programme in the disciplinary field of […]: in which way is the topic of your research embedded in the field of […] or one of its sub-fields?

7 Further information/comments/suggestions

Appendix E
The Rough Topic Exploration
In-class assignment, Session 1

The Rough Topic Exploration Matrix, in-class assignment

'In the next 30 minutes, you will make your first move on the chessboard of the topic exploration. The core idea is that you will organize your topic exploration in a very systematic, one could say, scientific way. You could see it as a little research project on its own. To facilitate this first step, we have developed an overview of the various sources of inspiration you could dispose of in delineating your scientific interests.

The matrix mentions several information sources. We ask you to write down which possibilities you are considering for contacting, reading, analysing. Do not misunderstand this invitation: you are not asked to take a hasty decision about your topic. We only want you to think in a systematic way about the strategies you will use in developing concrete and more specific ideas about a research topic.

Together with the Snapshot we will discuss this form during the individual feedback sessions on …'

The Rough Topic Exploration Matrix

You may hand this in at the end of the first Lab session, or you may take it home to think it over again and turn it into a digital version you will send to the lecturers one week before the individual meeting.

Name: _____

Table 6.3 The Rough Topic Exploration Matrix

Analyse your social interests, activities outside your formal study programme (voluntary work, jobs, political involvement). Write down in the right column if one or some of them could be functional with respect to taking a decision about your research topic.

Think about your papers, reports, journal articles and theses you have written: are there 'red threads of preferences' as regards specific substantive issues, location or period of research, methods of research, type of research?

Meeting peers is especially important in developing your topic interests. Which peers, outside and inside the programme, would be good sparring partners?

Analysing research environments, reading research programmes and meeting possible supervisors ('hunters' as well as 'sleeping beauties') are all especially useful steps in the topic exploration. What concrete ideas come to mind in thinking about these sources of inspiration and information?

Doing some literature search 'light' will give you a first insight into the state of the art of the academic thinking about topics. We will train you in doing a proper literature review, but can you formulate already now some literature sources you could consult in this first exploration?

Finally, we suggest considering the possibility of looking at a concrete case or example in your fields of interest. It will make potential topics much more palpable. Is this an option for you? Explain your yes or no.

Appendix F

Planning the well-reasoned topic choice and proposal design

In-class assignment, Session 2

1 Students indicate in which week(s) they will work on the respective activities.

Table 6.4 Proposal Lab activity timetable

Activity	Week 1	2	3	4	5	6	7	8	9	10
Evaluation of your approach of the topic exploration										
Analysis of your previous study and research activities										
Consultation of experts										
possible supervisors										
peers										
Search and analysing of literature										
Studying case material, examples										
Starting research file										
A comparative strength/weakness analysis of the various topics										
Studying literature on designing a research project										
Writing a paragraph about what you learned from the literature on designing a research project										
Taking a decision on the topic										

(Continued)

Table 6.4 (Continued)

Activity	Week 1	2	3	4	5	6	7	8	9	10
Taking a decision on the context of topic (Master's thesis, PhD project)										
Taking a decision on the location of execution of research										
Taking a decision on supervisor										
Start writing draft of well-reasoned topic choice (WRTC)										
Finishing draft WRTC										
Discussion of draft WRTC										
Finishing WRTC										
Handing in WRTC										x

2 Students indicate the timing of the proposal development.

Table 6.5 Timing of proposal development

Activity	Month 1	2	3	4	5	6	7	8
1. Starting and keeping my research file								
1. Making proposal planning with supervisor								
2. Deciding with supervisor about milestones and deadlines for assessing work in progress								

(Continued)

Table 6.5 (Continued)

Activity	Month 1	2	3	4	5	6	7	8
3. Milestones for progress evaluation								
4. Taking care of funding issues								
5. Exploration of topic								
6. Turning topic into first version of questions								
7. Review of literature								
8. Explorative research								
9. Reformulation of questions								
10. Choice of (sample of) objects to be studied								
11. Deciding which data need to be collected								
12. Deciding which methods of data collection are appropriate								
13. Design of research project (conceptual and technical)								

(Continued)

Table 6.5 (Continued)

Activity	Month 1	2	3	4	5	6	7	8
14. Final version research proposal (in view of go/no-go decision)								
15. Approval of proposal by supervision team								
16. Buffer time								+ + + +

Appendix G

Proposal information and tips

Session 3

Table of contents:

1 Writing the proposal abstract
2 Rubrics for evaluating the proposal qualities
3 Criteria for evaluating research questions

1 Writing the proposal abstract

The usefulness of proposals is greatly enhanced if their contents are summarized by a short, descriptive title and a well-written abstract. These are the starting points that enable evaluators to decide on subsidizing and acceptance of PhD projects.

What constitutes a good abstract?

An abstract of a proposal is a collection of statements that comprises the essential points of the document. It should be informative and present as much as possible of the quantitative or qualitative information contained in the article. In the case of our programme, it should be between 200 and 250 words long (usually 100–150 words), or as short as possible without omitting essential information or endangering its accuracy. It should state (Brewer, 2007: 132):

1 what is presented, theorized, studied
2 the purpose and context of the research
3 theories used to explain what will be reported
4 the hypotheses, which will be tested, and/or the leading research question and the sub-questions which the research project will attempt to answer
5 what the sample(s) or units/subjects of study will be
6 how data will be collected and analysed (the research methods used)
7 the relevance of the research project to the field of study.

How to prepare your abstract

- Read the draft of your proposal, and list, in order, the topics that are discussed.
- Review each topic in turn to see if direct informative statements of the specificities of the topic can be written.
- Compose a first sentence that will clearly establish the context and scope of the proposal.
- Edit the completed abstract for style. Use definite statements instead of generalities. Use the shortest clear expression for each thought.
- Do mention important authors or theories that are crucial to the understanding of your work.

Check that the abstract meets these four criteria:

- The abstract tells the prospective reader what the proposal is about, in language appropriate to the field.
- The abstract states the principal purposes of the proposal.
- The abstract is no longer than necessary, in this case 200–250 words.
- The abstract does not contain concepts or purposes beyond those discussed or arrived at in the proposal itself.

Examples

For some good and many bad (!) examples of thesis abstracts, consult relevant internet sites.

Conclusion

An abstract, by its content, form and style, should preview the rest of the proposal. The abstract is often the only part of a proposal that will ever be examined by colleagues or researchers. That abstract will be used to decide if its research proposal will be ignored or if it merits further attention.

2. Rubrics for evaluating the proposal qualities

This part of the Proposal Information (Oost et al., 2008) will give your students an insight in the evaluation criteria that play a significant role in the final assessment of their proposal.

> Basic rating scale
>
> 1= blank/unacceptable, 2 = needs improvement, 3 = satisfactory, 4 = good, 5 = excellent

A Abstract

Relevant elements

Research problem (including intended domain), actual subjects or entities (domain to be achieved), function (e.g., describing, explaining) and structure of the research (main sub-questions), data collection and data analysis methods (design), and expected results (possible answer).

> **Rubric**
>
> 1= Lack of abstract/essentially incomplete overview of the proposal.
> 2= Overview of the proposal lacking information on either research problem or function and structure or data-collection.
> 3= Overview of the proposal adequately summarizing some of the relevant research elements. However, information on research problem, function and structure, and data collection is included.
> 4= Overview of the proposal adequately summarizing most of the relevant research elements, including information on research problem, function and structure, and data collection.
> 5= Overview of the proposal adequately summarizing all the relevant research elements concerned.

B Research problem

Relevant elements

Research problem (formulating the most important question the research must answer) and most important sub-questions.

> **Rubric**
>
> 1= Lacking information on most important question and sub-questions derived from the research problem.
> 2= Summary of research problem (most important question) and most important sub-questions.
> 3= Satisfactory overview of most important question, sub-questions.
> 4= Logically organized overview of most important question, sub-questions, and aspired contribution to the discipline.
> 5= Logically organized and excellent communicated overview of most important question, sub-questions, and aspired contribution to the field.

C Motivation

Relevant elements

Argument for the newsworthiness, theoretical and/or practical or social relevance, and scope of the research problem (originality, relevance).

Rubric

1= Lack of justification/Justification section *lacking* an arguable position in outline.
2= Justification arguing for the newsworthiness and relevance of the research problem, *needing greater care* in documenting sources, greater effort into organizing the text and/or a deeper level of analysis.
3= Selective literature review *adequately substantiating* that the research problem has not yet been answered sufficiently (newsworthiness) and contributes to science (theoretical relevance) and/or society (practical/social relevance). Information on the scope of the research problem may be limited.
4= Selective and critical literature review *effectively substantiating* that the research problem has not yet been answered sufficiently (newsworthiness) and contributes to science (theoretical relevance) and/or society (practical/social relevance). Information on the scope of the research problem may be limited.
5= Selective and critical literature review *effectively substantiating* that the research problem has not yet been answered sufficiently (newsworthiness), contributes to science (theoretical relevance) and/or society (practical/social relevance), and cannot yield more information, given the subject, conditions and the research context (scope). *Clear information on the scope of the research, clearly showing 'the bigger story' behind the specific topic.*

D Theory

Relevant elements

'Theoretical context' including the research's position in the specialist field/s (particularly in relation to other research), research theme/s contained in the problem, choices and presuppositions concerning the subject matter, rationale for these choices and presuppositions, and definitions of the main concepts. Contribution to the disciplinary state of the art.

Rubric

1= Lack of theoretical context/Theory section *lacking* an arguable theoretical position in outline. Documentation is poorly constructed or absent. Aspired contribution to the discipline not mentioned.

2= Theory section clarifying in outline the theoretical context of the research, *needing greater care* in documenting sources, greater effort into organizing the text and/or a deeper level of analysis. Information on the aspired contribution to the discipline is not included.
3= Selective literature review *adequately clarifying some* of the relevant elements of the research context. Indications with respect to the possible contribution to the discipline.
4= Selective and critical literature review *effectively clarifying most* of the relevant elements of the research context, *formulating a tentative position with respect to the aspired contribution to the discipline*.
5= Selective and critical literature review, *effectively clarifying all* the relevant elements of the research context, *formulating a clear and robust position with respect to the aspired contribution to the discipline*.

E Methods and Research Design

Relevant elements

- Function of the research (describing, comparing, defining, evaluating, explaining, designing)
- Sample (segment of the population [universe of units or objects] that is selected for research, for example locations, periods, objects, actors, etc.)
- The properties or attributes of object(s) of research (to be compared, described, evaluated, etc.).
- Data collection methods.

Rubric

1= Lack of methods section/methods section showing hardly any information on research function, sample, object properties and methods.
2= Methods section lacking relevant information on the research function, sample, object properties and methods, and/or level of analysis needs improvement.
3= Methods section adequately clarifying research function, sample, object properties and methods. Level of analysis is satisfactory but is lacking details in motivation.
4= Methods section effectively clarifying research function, sample, object properties and methods. Level of analysis and motivation is good.
5= Methods section effectively clarifying research function, sample, object properties and methods. Level of analysis and motivation is excellent.

F References

Relevant elements

Bibliography, Information on search strategy with respect to bibliography.

> **Rubric**
>
> 1= *Lack of* bibliography. Information on search strategy *absent*/Bibliography lacking proper format and limited details with many sources missing or incomplete. Search strategy displaying *minimal effort* in selecting quality resources.
> 2= Bibliography showing *some errors* in generally accepted disciplinary format with *most sources shown* and a limited variety of sources. Search strategy displaying that the researcher *could have put greater effort* in selecting quality resources.
> 3= Bibliography showing *no errors* in generally accepted disciplinary format with *all sources shown* and an acceptable variety of sources. Search strategy displaying a *moderately systematic* way of gathering information.
> 4= Bibliography showing *no errors* in generally accepted disciplinary format with *all sources shown* and a rather wide variety of sources. Search strategy displaying a *mainly systematic* way of gathering information.
> 5= Bibliography showing *no errors* in generally accepted disciplinary format with *all sources shown* and a wide variety of sources. Search strategy displaying an *extremely systematic* way of gathering information.

G Consistency

Relevant elements

(Consistency check by the reviewer.) Relationships between research problem, motivation, theory and methods; relationships between paragraphs within these sections.

> **Rubric**
>
> 1= Lack of relevant information making a consistency check inappropriate/ Proposal showing hardly any consistency between the research problem, the motivation, the theory and/or the methods section. Documentation is poorly constructed or absent. Text lacks clear and logical development of ideas with no transition between ideas and paragraphs.
> 2= Proposal seldom showing consistency between the research problem, the motivation, the theory and the methods section. Development of

ideas is slightly clear, logical and thorough with weak transition between the paragraphs in sections.
3= Proposal usually showing consistency between the research problem, the motivation, the theory and the methods section. Development of ideas is moderately clear, logical, and thorough with adequate transition between the three paragraphs.
4= Proposal always showing consistency between the research problem, the motivation, the theory and the methods section. Connections between the relevant research elements are clear but not always explicit. Development of ideas is mainly clear, logical and thorough with good transition between paragraphs.
5= Proposal always showing consistency between the research problem, the motivation, the theory and the methods section. Connections between the relevant research elements are clear and always explicit. Development of ideas is extremely clear, logical, mature and thorough with excellent transition between the three paragraphs.

H Reflection

Relevant elements

One page annex to the Proposal (Halfway) (not being part of the proposal itself!), clarifying the author's appreciation of the strengths and weaknesses of the proposal and the planned action of improvement between, for example, 1 May and 15 June.

Rubric

1= Lack of reflection/Reflection demonstrating lack of interest in proposal's strengths and weaknesses, and possible improvements.
2= Reflection somewhat superficially considering proposal's strengths and weaknesses, and possible improvements.
3= Reflection adequately considering proposal's strengths and weaknesses, and possible improvements.
4= Reflection accurately considering proposal's strengths and weaknesses, and possible improvements.
5= Reflection excellently evaluating proposal's strengths and weaknesses, and possible improvements.

3 Criteria for evaluating research questions

Research questions for a thesis or project (Bryman, 2008: 33):

1 Should be clear, understandable to you and others.
2 Should be researchable, being capable of development into a research design.

3 Should connect with established theory and research.
4 Should be linked with each other.
5 Should have potential for contributing to knowledge.
6 Should be neither too broad nor too narrow.

Avoid, for example:

1 Questions whose answers are settled fact you could just look up.
2 Questions that will not be answerable because you cannot imagine finding hard data that might settle the question.
3 Questions …
   a based on preference or taste.
   b that force the researcher to read too many sources.
   c whose answers ask for crucial sources that are unattainable.
   d whose answer you cannot disprove (Booth et al., 2016).

Checklist for the elaboration into sub-questions

1 Will the answers to the sub-questions yield all the information necessary for answering the main research question? No vital questions forgotten?
2 Is every question necessary in answering the main research question? Is every answer contributing to the conclusion? No redundancies?
3 Have the sub- and sub-sub-questions been elaborated in a consistent, coherent way? Will they yield a consistent overall image of the situation under study?

Appendix H
A well-reasoned topic choice
Guidelines for students and PhD candidates

After about 2½ months, you will complete your 'topic exploration'. You will write a paper entitled 'A well-reasoned topic choice'. This paper has the following components:

1 An Introduction containing information on the following points:
   a The importance for the author of the topic exploration.
   b The way in which the author has come to the choice of topics which have been researched in detail.
   c The sources that were used for the exploration of the topics.
2 The approach of the 'topic exploration' and your evaluation of the approach: what went well?, where did you meet problems?, how did you solve them?
3 What do five obvious 'sources of inspiration' tell you about the possible topics?
   a Your own previous study and research activities.
   b Experts, possible supervisors, peers, etc.
   c The literature.
   d Studied case material and examples, your own social experiences.
   e Your personal 'research file'.
4 A comparative strength/weakness analysis of the various topics that you have examined and considered.
5 A paragraph on what you took from the literature your teacher has suggested to you for reading as regards developing your research objective and research perspective.
6 Conclusion
   a Which topic do you choose after careful consideration? (This choice reflects your ideas and thinking per end of December. In the months that will follow, your ideas might change. That is a natural thing.)
   Write a paragraph that starts with formulating your topic in conformity with the following format. You would like to explain or elaborate your

text under 1, 2 and 3. But start with forcing yourself to write according to this format.

Format (indicating what you do not know or understand about your topic) (suggestion Booth et al.. 2016):

1. I am studying/working on ....
....
2. because I want to find out who/what/when/where/whether/why/how ....
....
3. to help my reader understand better ....
....

  b The function of the proposal. Will it be developed in view of Master's thesis, or PhD proposal, or an application for an internal or external PhD position, or will it be written as a 'stand-alone' exercise in writing a proposal?

  c Location of the research.

  d Supervision/mentorship: who can supervise and advise you in the process of the proposal writing?

  e Issues that are still open, points which you wish to discuss with the Proposal Lab convener(s).

7. The paper (between 2500 and 3000 words) contains a bibliography of 20 texts (articles, book chapters, books) you consider to be closely related to your topic.

8. Deadline: as agreed with the convener of the Proposal Lab and/or supervisor.

Appendix I

Instructions in form format for writing the Proposal Halfway

Maximum 2000 words
Name:_____
Title of the project: _____

1 Give a brief description of your project

Explanation

Usually, this part of a proposal is called The Abstract. In this case, it should be between 200 and 250 words long (usually 100–150 words), or as short as possible without omitting essential information or endangering its accuracy. It should state:

1. what is presented, theorized, studied
2. the purpose and context of the research
3. theories used to explain what will be reported
4. the hypotheses, which will be tested, or/and the leading research question and the sub questions which the research project will attempt to answer
5. what the sample(s) or units/subjects of study will be
6. how data will be collected and analysed (the research methods used)
7. the relevance of the research project to the field of study.

2 The research question

a *Description of the field of study and the existing body of knowledge with reference to that.* What don't we know and understand? What has been neglected? What is the central object of the proposed research? And what is the research objective? Try as hard as you can to formulate your research interests in terms of a conceptual problem, in terms of what we don't know or understand, in terms of something that we want to make understandable for others. Don't focus to early on practical problems, things you want to solve in the practical sense.

Explanation

This part of the paper is directly inspired by what you have read in the literature, the interviews you held, the meetings you had with your (possible supervisor), and what you wrote down in other assignments. In particular, the literature review will be of great value.

You can be sure that those texts contain sentences you are very pleased with, expressing exactly where you like to focus on. Use them! In this section you analyse the state of the research *à propos* your topic. Essentially, this section is laying the foundation for your questions, your interest. The character of this section is an evaluation of what has already been researched as regards your topic.

b *The core question.* Which central question would you like to answer with the research? How do you unfold the central question into sub-questions, so that the joint answers will generate the answer to the central question?

Explanation

Take provisional decisions about the type of research questions you like to answer (in correspondence with your research objective). Core qualities of good questions (Bryman, 2008) are:

- Clear to you and others.
- Being researchable.
- There should be literature on which you can draw to help illuminate how your research question should be approached.
- Being able to contribute to topic knowledge.
- Being neither too broad nor too narrow.

The questions should have a steering function, indicating what different types of knowledge are required and what material needs to be gathered (Verschuren and Doorewaard, 2005).

3 The innovative character of the proposed project

What is the significance of your thesis? Does it contain an original contribution to the field of existing knowledge? Is it of specific social or theoretical relevance?

Explanation

The originality and relevance of a project can take many forms (Guetzkow, Lamont and Mallard, 2004): an original approach, an understudied area, an original topic, an original theory, an original method, original data, original results.

You can specify these main types of originality by asking yourself questions such as: will I formulate new questions?, will I study aspects of my topic that have been understudied until now?, will I bring together theoretical insights in an unexpected way?, will I bring together methods in an unexpected way?

4 Considerations regarding theory and prior research

Sketch of the *dominant theoretical approaches* and debates that will inspire your ambitions to answer your research questions. Which scholars in your field do you find especially relevant to your research objectives work?

Explanation

The foundation for all this information is lying in your literature search, literature notes, critical appraisal and literature review.

In this section you will explain from which perspective you will try to answer your research questions, for example, explaining the theoretical foundations for a hypothesis, a research argument, a claim.

In view of this assignment, we use the following working definition of theory. A theory is a collection of well-motivated, disciplinary embedded and researchable propositions/theses that try to explain or try to understand, for example, the existence or non-existence of a problem, the similarities and differences between A&B [etc.], the appropriateness of a normative position, the (in)effectiveness of a measure, the plausibility of a development.

5 Proposition, hypotheses and concepts

What is the central proposition? Your argument? Which are the working hypotheses? What are the main theoretical concepts you intend to use?

6 The data and methods

Describe the empirical data, the sources, the documents to be used for answering each of the research questions. How do you intend to gather your data? Do you have whatever permission might be required? Have the necessary informants agreed to co-operate? Do you have access to the archives you need?

7 Additional information

a Who will be your supervisor of the research project you are preparing with this Proposal (Halfway)?
b List your publications that are relevant to the project.
c Provide a short and provisional bibliography of between 15 and 20 titles.

Provide concise and clear answers, based on the ideas and information you have at the moment of handing it in. When new data and theoretical insights become available, you may have other ideas and your plans may change accordingly. We will discuss your Proposal Halfway on ...., or earlier if you like working on your Proposal ahead of the Proposal Lab scheme. You will hand in the Final Proposal on ...

Having arrived at this point in your Proposal Halfway, you will heave a deep sigh of relief. Let it rest for a couple of days, re-read it, make some more improvements ... and then ... send it to your evaluators!

Appendix J

The disciplinary embedding assignment

Session 4 and Session 5

Disciplinary embedding: area/theme/subject/ essential others

To be sent to the Proposal Lab conveners before ....

In preparation for the session on disciplinary embedding, you will write down your research area, a specific research theme and your provisional research topic. In this assignment, we ask you to try and fill out a complete 'specification'. This can be done by working either 'top-down' (starting from your research subject) or 'bottom-up' (beginning at the topic of your research). (In most cases, you will use both methods.)

Please write down your specification on this form. Try to follow the specification steps of:

- discipline;
- disciplinary subfield;
- your theme;
- essential 'others' (fellow researchers);
- their debates;
- remaining questions (in your view, in the opinion of other authors);
- your niche for doing something relevant, original;
- theoretical anchor points, as offered by other authors;
- your subject.

In case your subject is located at the meeting point of several disciplines, first clarify which disciplines are involved and how your research is anchored in those disciplines. If you will be working in more than one discipline, you will do the specification two times. Find out if researchers work at the meeting point of two or more disciplines on a subject that overlaps with your own interest.

We realize that issues 6, 7 and 8 (see below) can be difficult at this moment. You may keep these in reserve for the December meeting on the well-reasoned topic choice. But if you dare to try it now, we will gladly give feedback!

Name: _____

1. * Discipline (s)
2. * Sub-discipline
3. * [Sub-sub-discipline]
4. * The themes in your discipline that interests you
5. * Essential others (in view of your research theme or topic). Rely on your journal search. Who are the most important authors for you? You could try to find two authors with whom you agree and two with whom you disagree. Explain your choice.
6. If possible: Their debates, their creative agreements, their creative disagreements …
7. If possible: … and their theories (theoretical, analytical, interpretative, explanatory frameworks) of relevance for the theme under study.
8. If possible: Remaining questions, research issues (in your view, in the opinion of other authors)
9. Your niche for doing something relevant, original (as you feel this moment)
10. Your provisional topic:

Appendix K

The Question Practicum

Session 6

Name:_____

Let's assume you are very close to taking a decision on a well-reasoned topic choice. Please indicate in Table 6.6 what your preferences with respect to your research objective are. If appropriate, feel free to mark and explain more than one option. Table 6.7 presents the types of choices available.

Table 6.6 Your research perspective preference and your choices

Research perspectives	Motivation
Theory-developing research	
Theory-testing research	
Problem-finding research	
Diagnostic research	
Evaluation research	

Table 6.7 Types of questions

Type of question	Examples	Your research question	Possible sub-questions
Type 1. Existence questions	'Does x exist?' Important when (non-)existence of something is controversial' (Meltzoff, 2007)		1. 2. 3. etc.

(Continued)

Table 6.7 (Continued)

Type of question	Examples	Your research question	Possible sub-questions
Type 2. Questions of Description, Classification and Composition	'What is x like? Is it variable or invariant? …. What are the components that make up x?' (Meltzoff, 2007) 'What are its qualities, what characteristics does it have? How is it? What is it made of? Who or what does it involve? What does it look like?' (Oost, 2003)		1. 2. 3. etc.
3. Descriptive-comparative questions	'What are the differences? What are the similarities? In what ways are they different? In what ways do they overlap, are they the same?' (Oost, 2003)		1. 2. 3. etc.
Explanatory knowledge. Questions of relationship and explanation.			
4. Relationship questions	'Is there a relationship between x and y?' (Meltzoff, 2007)		1. 2. 3. etc.
5. Causality questions	'Why is it so? How did it happen? What is this a consequence of? What reasons are there? What is its background? How could this happen?' (Oost, 2003)		1. 2. 3. etc.
Evaluative knowledge			
6. Questions of Evaluation	'What is its worth? How well does it work? … What are its advantages and disadvantages?' (Meltzoff, 2007)		1. 2. 3. etc.
Alternative types of questions			
7. Other types of questions you consider			

Checklist for the elaboration into sub-questions

1. Is every question formulated in a transparent way? Are all concepts clear and operational?
2. Will the answers to the questions yield all the information necessary for answering the main (central, one-and-only, final) research question? No vital questions forgotten?
3. Is every question necessary for answering the main research question!!!!!!!!!!!!? Does every answer contribute to the conclusion? No redundancies?
4. Have the sub- and sub-sub-questions been elaborated in a consistent, coherent way? Will they yield a consistent overall image of the situation under study?
5. Will you be able to answer all these questions in the time given?

What have been the greatest problems you encountered when turning your research interests into the format of questions?

Appendix L
Evaluating individual research training assignments

1 Evaluation of interview reports

We assess the reports of the interviews on the following aspects:

1. Substantive value of the interview. Does it contain important substantive information about
   a. the subject itself, but also about the response of the interviewee as regards
   b. the subject being a good option for a Master's Thesis or PhD project?
2. Information on the preparation of the interview:
   a. Overview of questions asked.
   b. The way the interviewee was informed. For example, via the text of an email message inviting the interviewee for the interview, or sending information about the research plans of the interviewer.
   c. The way the interviewer had collected information about the interviewee.
3. The relationship between the interviewer and interviewee:
   a. Was the interviewer 'on par' with the interviewee, not only requesting information, but also providing information?
   b. Did the interviewer have concrete research plans that could be exchanged?
4. Reflection on the interview, lessons that can be drawn for subsequent occasions.
5. The quality of the report as a written document:
   a. Clear structure, use of subheadings.
   b. Detailed in substantive information.
   c. A narrative structure.
   d. Good combination of summary passages and quotes.
   e. It is also well defensible if the student reports in the form of a literal transcription?
6. Is evidence shown of having studied the methodological literature on interviewing?

Some observations

The quality of the interview strongly depends on the stage of the student's choice of subject. Students who do not yet have a grip on their subject are very dependent on the interviews and are more the requesting party than formulating research suggestions to which they would like to receive a response. Their attitude has something of a submissiveness, they are consuming and not producing.

A particularly good report looks like this.

> Primarily, the report is intrinsically interesting to read. As readers we really learn from it. This is partly because the students are not too concise in reporting. If the self-defensible literal transcription of the interview is not chosen, the students will find a nice balance between the summary of the conversation and the use of appealing quotes. The students succeed well in bringing the interviewee's reactions to the fore in a clear manner. The students prepared the interview very well by informing the interviewee in advance about the issues that the interview would discuss. Sometimes the students have already sent a summary of their research ideas. It is also particularly good if the students show that they have studied publications by the interviewee before the interview. The students reflect well on the preparation of the interview, the progress (what went well, what went badly) and the relationship that developed with the interviewee. It is extra nice if the students occasionally connect this to the literature they read about interviewing. The report shows that the students actively contributed their own plans to the interview. There was talk of equal interlocutors. It was a conversation 'on a high level'. The report makes it clear what the value of the interview has been in view of taking decisions on the research topic. The report contains at least three parts: overview of the preparation, including the interview questions; substantive report of what was discussed; reflection on the preparation, progress and results of the interview. We also need to be able to determine from the interview report whether the interview went well in all probability. A nice added value also arises if the students can place several interviews in a mutually comparative context, showing different views on the same issue.

2 Evaluation of the literature search report

A good report on the literature search will contain the following elements:

- The result: the articles and books that are key publications. Are there 15–20? Or more?
- Information on the diversity of literature sources. Has one also looked at sources other than just electronic (also consultation of experts, library visits)?

- An overview of the inclusion and exclusion criteria the student has used in determining which sources will be researched (quality level of journals, periods, language, etc.).
- A feeling for a not-too-narrow definition of inclusion and exclusion criteria.
- Ability to be flexible regarding including and excluding literature.
- The search terms used.
- How one has stored findings (Endnote, for example). Indication that the author has a feeling for the available possibilities to record results (RefWorks, End Note).
- Role of the literature search in the future of the research that is being done. Understanding the iterative character of the literature search. Indications that the author continues to search.
- A feeling for the issue of synonyms and language differences. Understanding that different terms might relate to the same subject.
- The presence of an Introduction, including the leading question that steers the literature search.
- Presentation of the search terms that have been used.
- An overview of consulted databases.
- Clear and convincing criteria for determining the relevance of a publication.
- The ability to recognize the strengths and weaknesses of the search strategy and its results.

3 Evaluation of the critical appraisals

Checklist for reviewing publications, based on a compilation of checkpoints as presented by Greenhalgh (2010) (Table 6.8).

Table 6.8 Checkpoints for a literature review

Checkpoints to determine what the publication is about	Answer
1. Why was the study done (what question did it address)?	
2. Did the publication address an important question?	

3. What type of study was done?
  a. Primary research
  b. Secondary research	

Checkpoints for the methods section of the paper	
4. Is a method section part of the paper?	

(Continued)

Table 6.8 (Continued)

Checkpoints to determine what the publication is about	Answer
5. What methods did the researcher use for collecting data – and are these described in enough detail?	
6. Was the study design appropriate to the broad field of research addressed?	
7. Was the methodological approach appropriate?	
8. Was a thorough search done of the appropriate literature?	
9. Whom or what is the study about?	
a. How were settings, participants and objects selected?	
b. Who, what was included in, and who, what was excluded from the study?	
10. Has the author determined whether settings, participants, cases, objects are comparable?	
11. What kind of data has the author collected?	

Checkpoints for robustness of publication

12. Has the material been published in an independent peer-reviewed journal or book?
13. Has any significant evidence or argument been omitted from this publication?
14. Has author-bias been avoided?
15. What was the researcher's perspective, and has this been considered?
16. How sensitive are the results to the way the research has been done?
17. Did the publication involve a significant conflict of interests?

Checkpoints for evaluating the results

18. Are the results credible, and if so, are they scientifically important?
19. What conclusions were drawn, and are they justified by the results?
20. Are the findings of the study transferable to other settings?

Checkpoint for further research

21. What further research does the author believe is needed, and is this justified?

Questions:

1 Are all the elements of this checklist discussed in the report?
2 Is the relationship made with one's own research?
3 Does the author succeed in interrelating multiple critical appraisals (comparative strength/weakness analysis of the two articles discussed)?
4 Is the quality of the writing in order?

In summary, we could distinguish the following quality levels in the critical appraisals:

- Acceptable (6). Shows that the author has followed the points of attention as formulated in Appendix L, Evaluation of the critical appraisals'. But does that very succinctly and shows little critical judgement. The quality of the writing and the layout of the paper are just acceptable.
- More than sufficient (7). The author deals with all the items of the form, is critical, substantiates the criticism but gives little information about the content of the articles studied.
- Good (8). Follows all items of the form, critically assesses, substantiates the opinion, writes in an informative way about the articles and the quality of the writing is good.
- Very good (9). Is critical in all respects. The criticism is well founded. Provides a lot of substantive information about the publication. Uses a comparative perspective and relates the publications to their own research. The paper is well written.

Red flags while writing a critical appraisal

Make students aware that if they use words (and they will!) like: 'I feel', 'I am quite sure', 'I believe', 'I do not have the feeling that', 'I cannot tell for sure', 'it is my feeling', 'my intuitive guess is'… they should immediately ask themselves whether they can substantiate that conclusion properly.

4 The evaluation of a literature review

A literature review consists of the following elements (with an indication of evaluation criteria) (Table 6.9).

Table 6.9 Elements of a literature review

Dimensions	Presentation of research questions that lead literature review
	Showing the importance of the review and why the reader needs to read it
	Roadmap for reader of literature review
Component	*Literature review*
Dimensions	Comprehensive
	Up to date
	Shows critical and analytical thinking about the literature, so not just being a summary of what has been read
	Command of the literature
	Selectivity, discriminating between important and unimportant works
	Thematic structuring
	Alignment with research question
	Showing strengths and limitations of literature
Component	*Discussion/conclusion*
Dimensions	Summary
	Refers to introduction
	Ties everything together
	Implications and applications for author's own research
Evaluation aspect	*Presentation, quality of writing*
Dimensions	Broken up the text in paragraphs with appropriate subheadings
	No excessive use of jargon
	Not quoting excessively when presenting the literature
	Fully acknowledged the work of others

A good literature review shows a critical appraisal of the literature. This means students will assess the articles and books from a peer review perspective.

They will indicate the strong and weak aspects of the work in question in terms of quality and methodology, the type of research that is used, whether there is a sharp problem and a clear research question, whether the research question is answered.

Appendix M
SWOT analysis by candidates already halfway to a proposal (the Clinic)

Table 6.10 SWOT analysis of proposal-half way

Your knowledge of supervisor's expectations regarding:	**Strength**	**Weakness**	Your skills, your knowledge:

1. Timing of project
2. Length of your appointment/scholarship
3. Format of the thesis:
  a. Coherence important?
  b. Number of articles
  c. Status of journals
4. Evaluation criteria in view of proposal
5. Who will be the evaluators?
			1. How to plan
			2. How to work with flowcharts
			3. How to get from topic to question
			4. Literature search
			5. Critical appraisal of literature
			6. Characteristics of a literature review
			7. Role of theory / hypothesis / claim in the proposal

Your feeling as regards congruence between supervisors (for example, in view of expectations)	**Opportunity**	**Threat**	8. The Proposal Format 9. Research design in your discipline 10. Quality criteria applying to proposal 11. How to make an original contribution
Your knowledge of financial conditions			12. 80 per cent ready model 13. Proficiency in English 14. Managing supervisors
Your knowledge of agreements regarding (co-)authorship			
Other information issues.......			Other skills............

Appendix N
Expectations in view of a 4 year PhD project

The overview is based on a PhD trajectory of 4 years. In case of 'dual' or 'external' candidates (with no employee status as a PhD candidate and working part-time on their project), we depart from a multiplier of 1.5 (i.e., a PhD trajectory of 6 years). The overview has been composed based on advice by supervisors working in the technical and educational disciplines. It must be adapted to the requirements of your own discipline and field of research (Table 6.11).

Table 6.11 Timetable for 4 year PhD project

Monitoring moment	Required	Material on behalf of the evaluation
At the end of the first year (in case of full-time trajectory) or after 1 ½ years (in case of part-time trajectory)	In co-operation with the supervisor/advisor, the PhD candidate is formulating realistic expectations regarding the PhD trajectory (who will be my readers?, will I author my thesis as a monograph?, will my thesis consist of articles?, what is my post-PhD career perspective?, how much time do I have available for my thesis work?, what will I do next to my thesis work (for example, teaching, etc.)?	A note on expectations, written by the PhD candidate, co-signed by the supervisor/advisor

(Continued)

Table 6.11 (Continued)

	The PhD candidate has made the research into his/her own project, has developed a personal vision on the research project	a. A research design / proposal formulated by the PhD candidate him or herself, or b. An updated version of the original plan.
	The PhD candidate has an overview of the literature and can sketch the context of the research (what has been 'solved,' where are lying my possibilities for a relevant and original contribution)	Literature review (of books and journals)
	The PhD candidate is capable of the development and explication of the theoretical framework	
	The PhD candidate has control of the technical skills to execute the research	Written report about the technical execution of an experiment, a pilot study, etc.
	The PhD candidate has a budget for extra training	
	The PhD candidate is capable of the organization of the data collection	See research plan / proposal / design
	The PhD candidate has collected a first set of data and results	Report on results of experiment / test / pilot study / case study, etc. A ¾ version of a journal paper
	The PhD candidate has presented first results in his or her own research group or department	Written full text of the presentation (not only PowerPoint slides)
	The PhD candidate is participating actively in his or her research group	Presence + presentation

(Continued)

Table 6.11 (Continued)

	Optional	The PhD candidate has started to build his or her own network	
		PhD candidate is preparing himself or herself for teaching	Evidence of participation in course
		PhD candidate has presented first results outside the department	Written full text of the presentation (not only PowerPoint slides)
End of the second year (full-time), end third year (part-time)			
	Required		
		Increasingly the PhD candidate contributes independently to the project (proposes new actions, writes increasingly independently [the supervisor's contribution changes of character], proposes by own initiative topics for new papers	Shown, for example, in the discussion part of journal articles or in conference papers
		PhD candidate has collected his or her own data and analysed them autonomously	Report on results
		PhD candidate has received training in the writing of scientific papers	
		PhD candidate has drafted a report on his or her results	Paper or journal article I
		PhD candidate has presented his or her results (internally or externally)	Text of presentation (not only PowerPoint slides)
		PhD candidate has sought co-operation independently (internally and externally)	Report on behalf of supervisor

(*Continued*)

Table 6.11 (Continued)

		PhD candidate has made a time schedule for the completion of the thesis and is controlling the realization	Planning Matrix Regular reports on realization
	Optional		
		PhD candidate has prepared teaching	Evidence of participation in course
		PhD candidate has taught a course	
End of third year (full-time) / after 4.5 years (part-time)			
	Required	Candidate develops a personal view on research	Candidate starts co-developing a new research project with supervisor (for example in view of post-PhD career
		Candidate starts to get more knowledge on topic than supervisor	
		PhD candidate has collected his or her own data and analysed them autonomously	
		PhD candidate has drafted a report on his or results	Paper II and/or III
		PhD candidate has presented his or her results (externally)	Full text of presentation (not just the PowerPoint slides)
		Candidate has written first version of introduction chapter of thesis	Draft, presented to supervisors
		Candidate and supervisor exchange ideas about post-PhD career	Conversation

(Continued)

Table 6.11 (Continued)

		Candidate can conclude by himself or herself when a research activity can be considered to be completed	
	Desirable/ optional		
		Candidate has taught a course	
		Candidate and supervisor exchange ideas about new research (to be started after completion of thesis)	First note by candidate on application for new research grant
End of fourth year (full-time), after 6 years (part-time)			
	Required		
		Candidate develops personal view on research	Application for new research grant (if candidate wants to go on in research career)
		PhD candidate has presented results (externally)	Full text of introduction (not just PowerPoint slides)
		Completed the thesis	Handing in manuscript for final check by supervisors
	Desirable/ optional		
		Preparation of new research project	Application for subsidy with national or international research organization

Appendix O
Planning Matrix PhD trajectory
Research and other activities

Table 6.12 Planning the PhD journey

	First year				Second year				Third year				Fourth year			
	1st quarter	2nd	3rd	4th	1st	2nd	3rd	4th	1st	2nd	3rd	4th	1st	2nd	3rd	4th
Courses, substantive (disciplinary content)																
Courses, skills																
Definitive research Plan																
Handing in First year Training and Supervision Plan (see Appendix Q)																
Handing in Second year Training and Supervision Agreement																
Handing in Third year Training and Supervision Agreement																
Handing in Fourth year Training and Supervision Agreement																
Evaluation first year																
Evaluation second year																
Evaluation third year																
Evaluation fourth year																
Teaching																
Attending courses in preparation of teaching																

Article 1, submission
Article 2, submission
Article 3, submission (?)
Attending national conference
Attending international conference
Literature Review
Chapter on used methodologies (or methods section per article/chapter?)
Study visits abroad
Draft of introduction chapter
Definite version of Introduction
Finishing data collection
Chapter 2 (article 1?)
Chapter 3 (article 2?)
Chapter 4 (article 3?)
Chapter 5 (article 4?)
Concluding chapter
Thesis goes to supervisor for approval
Thesis goes to committee
Orientation as to post-PhD life

Appendix P

At the end of the proposal journey

SWOT Analysis in view of a (future) PhD project

Table 6.13 SWOT analysis in view of a (future) PhD project

Aspects to be considered in SWOT analysis	Strengths	Weaknesses	Aspects to be considered in SWOT analysis
• Quality of writing • Regularity of meetings with supervision team • Transparency of quality criteria used by supervisors • Planning of the project • Balance between project and other activities • Embedding in intellectual community (↔ isolation) • Disposal of research techniques (methods, writing notes, literature search, critical appraisal of sources, literature review techniques) • Ethical aspects of the project • Connection between prior training and qualities required by the project			• Knowing which sources or data are needed to answer the research questions • Having a view on the structure of the possible dissertation (remember Eco's provisional table of contents) • Planning of occasions where work in progress will be presented • Having the initiative in the preparation of meetings with supervisors • Demonstration of knowledge of the literature and its position in dissertation
	Opportunities	Threats	

(Continued)

Table 6.13 (Continued)

• Language proficiency (English) • Originality of the topic • Relevance of the topic • Grip on earlier scientific work regarding the topic • Quality of the primary research question • Ability to unfold primary research question into a set of sub-questions • Feeling for supervisor's expectations • Feeling for role of central research argument, claim, hypothesis • Having a grip on the concept of theory	• Clarity of the research problem • Clarity of concepts that are used • Grip on broader context of the topic • Grip on the history of your topic • Justification of chosen texts, sources, necessary data • Expertise in and availability of software that may be useful for data collection and data analysis • Locating the project in what has been done before • Ability to describe the project in a brief way (an abstract) • Ability to explain the project to non-specialists • Knowledge of sampling (selection of segment of sources, population, geographical or historical units for research)

Major worry in view of the project, at this moment:

Appendix Q

Training and supervision plan

Table 6.14 Important issues to be settled and evaluated regularly by PhD candidate and supervisor

Name of PhD candidate: _____
Name of supervisor: _____
Title of PhD project: _____
Date: _____

Task	Topic	Space for notes by PhD candidate and supervisor
1	Names of other supervisors/advisors involved in supervision of the project	
2	Do PhD candidate and supervisors have sufficient knowledge of regulations, codes of conduct, etc. in force at institute, graduate school where the PhD trajectory takes place? In other words: are PhD candidate and supervisors familiar with the local 'rules of the game'?	
3	Are changes in the supervision arrangement to be expected in view of departure or stay abroad of supervisors/advisors?	
4	(For foreign PhD candidates) Has a request for exemption of local exams been submitted and granted (for example, exemption of local Master's diploma after completion of Master's abroad)?	

(Continued)

Table 6.14 (Continued)

Task	Topic	Space for notes by PhD candidate and supervisor
5	Activities in prior period: – what were the planned activities? – which activities have been completed successfully? – reasons for non-completion (in case) – consequences for coming period	
6	Planning of research activities in coming period	
	Activity 1	
	Activity 2	
	Activity 3	
	Activity 4	
	Activity 5	
	Activity 6	
	Activity 7	
7	Have other activities been taken into account when making the research planning (teaching, preparation of teaching, conference visits, writing of articles, papers, pregnancy or parental leave, etc.)? Mention those other activities.	
8	Will the PhD candidate prepare himself or herself for the teaching by taking educational training?	
9	Have the financial preconditions for the PhD research been settled with the institutional authorities?	
10	Are infrastructure conditions okay (computer facilities, software, measurement equipment, etc.)?	
11	Have strengths and weaknesses of the PhD candidate been mapped or updated (in view of extra training or extra courses, etc.)? In case of desirable improvements, how will they be taken care of?	

(Continued)

Table 6.14 (Continued)

Task	Topic	Space for notes by PhD candidate and supervisor
12	Courses and extra training in next period	
13	Intentions with respect to meetings with peers, research group colleagues, consultation of external experts	
14	What are the agreements with respect to the progress evaluation in the coming period (content and procedure)? Think about: • Material to be handed in, for example, definite version of research proposal/design, literature review, conference paper, journal article, report on data collection, work planning for coming period, provisional table of contents of dissertation, chapters, etc. • Date on which the material will be handed in • Evaluators who will be involved in progress evaluation • Criteria that will be in force during the evaluation process	
15	When and in which journals will it be published?	
16	When will supervisor and PhD candidate communicate about post-PhD career options?	
17	Are the expectations with respect to the dissertation and the quality and quantity of research data transparent? What are the components of the dissertation, which criteria does the dissertation has to meet to be evaluated by the supervisor as acceptable, [very] good, etc.?	

(Continued)

Table 6.14 (Continued)

Task	Topic	Space for notes by PhD candidate and supervisor
18	What working agreements have been made between the PhD student and the (research) supervisor for the coming period (let's say, the coming year)? When and on which occasion will the PhD student and supervisor see each other?	Meeting 1, date....................; topic and product .... Meeting 2, date....................; topic and product .... Meeting 3, date....................; topic and product .... Meeting 4, date....................; topic and product .... Meeting 5, date....................; topic and product .... Meeting 6, date....................; topic and product .... Meeting 7, date....................; topic and product .... Meeting 8, date....................; topic and product .... Meeting 9, date....................; topic and product .... Meeting 10, date....................; topic and product ....

(Continued)

Table 6.14 (Continued)

Task	Topic	Space for notes by PhD candidate and supervisor
19	Considering the work to be done and/or evaluating the progress in the past period, what kind and intensity of supervision do PhD candidate and supervisor consider as optimal for the completion of the project?	

Bibliography

Allen, D.W. and Melnik, M.A. (1972) *The Development of a Clinic to Improve University Teaching by the School of Education at the University of Massachusetts (Amherst)*. Amherst, MA: University of Massachusetts, School of Education.
Aveyard, H. (2007) *Doing a Literature Review in Health and Social Care: A Practical Guide*. Maidenhead: Open University Press.
Becker, H.S. (1986) *Writing for Social Scientists: How to Start and Finish Your Thesis, Book, or Article*. Chicago: The University of Chicago Press.
Becker, H.S. (1998) *Tricks of the Trade: How to Think About Your Research While You're Doing It*. Chicago: The University of Chicago Press.
Bell, E., Bryman, A. and Harley, B. (n.d.) *Research Project Guide*. Oxford University Press. Available at: https://learninglink.oup.com/static/5bf28a25d910f40011b79ade/index.htm (accessed 23 Sept. 2021).
Booth, W.C., Colomb, G.G. and Williams. J.M. (2008) *The Craft of Research* (3rd edn). Chicago: The University of Chicago Press.
Booth, W.C., Colomb. G.G. Williams. J.M., Bizup, J. and FitzGerald, W.T. (2016) *The Craft of Research* (4th edn). Chicago: The University of Chicago Press.
Bordens, K.S. and Abbott, B.B. (2008) *Research Design and Methods*. New York: McGraw-Hill Higher Education.
Bowen, W.G. and Rudenstine, N.L. (1992) *In Pursuit of the PhD*. Princeton, NJ: Princeton University Press.
Brewer, R. (2007) *Your PhD Thesis: How to Plan, Draft, Revise and Edit Your Thesis*. Abergele: Studymates Limited.
Bryman, A. (2008) *Social Research Methods* (3rd edn). Oxford: Oxford University Press.
Colman, A.M. (2009) *Oxford Dictionary of Psychology*. Oxford: Oxford University Press.
Corbin, J, and Strauss, A. (2008) *Basics of Qualitative Research*. Los Angeles, CA: SAGE Publications.
Delamont, S., Atkinson, P. and Parry, O. (2004) *Supervising the Doctorate: A Guide to Success*. London: The Society for Research into Higher Education.
DiscoverPhDs (2021) PhD failure rate: A study of 26,076 PhD candidates. Available at: https://www.discoverphds.com/advice/doing/phd-failure-rate (accessed 6 Sept. 2021).
Eco, U. (1977) *Come si fa una tesi di laurea*. Milan: Bompiani.
Eco, U. (2005) *Hoe schrijf ik een scriptie* (12th edn). Amsterdam: Pockethuis in samenwerking met Uitgeverij Bert Bakker.
Eley, A.R. and Jennings, R. (2005) *Effective Postgraduate Supervision: Improving the Student/Supervisor Relationship*. Maidenhead: Open University Press.
Gage, N.L. (1972) *Teacher Effectiveness and Teacher Education: The Search for a Scientific Basis*. San Francisco, CA: Pacific Books.
Glaser, B.G. and Strauss, A.L. (2009) *The Discovery of Grounded Theory: Strategies for Qualitative Research*. New Brunswick, NJ: Aldine Transaction.
Gosling, P. and Noordam, B. (2006) *Mastering Your PhD: Survival and Success in the Doctoral Years and Beyond*. Berlin: Springer-Verlag.
Greenhalgh, T. (2010) *How to Read a Paper: The Basics of Evidence-Based Medicine* (4th edn). Oxford: Wiley-Blackwell.

Guetzkow, J., Lamont, M. and Mallard, G. (2004) What is originality in the social sciences and humanities?, *American Sociological Review* 69(2): 190–212. https://www.researchgate.net/publication/241644109_What_Is_Originality_in_the_Social_Sciences_and_the_Humanities

Hunt, J. and Nhlengethwa, S. (2009) *The Art of the Idea and How It Can Change Your Life*. New York: PowerHouse Books.

Lamont, M. (2009) *How Professors Think: Inside the Curious World of Academic Judgment*. Cambridge, MA: Harvard University Press.

Loehle, C. (2010) *Becoming a Successful Scientist: Strategic Thinking for Scientific Discovery*. Cambridge: Cambridge University Press.

Lovitts, B.E. (2001) *Leaving the Ivory Tower: The Causes and Consequences of Departure from Doctoral Study*. Lanham, MD: Rowman & Littlefield Publishers.

Lovitts, B.E. (2007) *Making the Implicit Explicit: Creating Performance Expectations for the Thesis*. Sterling, VA: Stylus Publishing.

Malmfors, B., Garnsworthy, P. and Grossman, M. (2002) *Writing and Presenting Scientific Papers*. Nottingham: Nottingham University Press.

Manathunga, C. (2005) Early warning signs in postgraduate research education: A different approach to ensuring timely completions. *Teaching in Higher Education*, 10: 219–33.

Meltzoff, J. (2007) *Critical Thinking About Research: Psychology and Related Fields* (9th edn). Washington, DC: American Psychological Association.

Mirande, M.J.A. (1986) De student als beginnend onderzoeker, doctoral thesis. University of Amsterdam.

Mohd Tahir, A. and Asmuni, A. (2016) Community of practice in doctoral education. Paper presented at Graduate Research in Education Seminar (GREDuc 2016), Universiti Putra Malaysia, Selangor, 17 December (pp. 464–70). Serdang: Faculty of Educational Studies, UPM.

Okorocha, E. (2007) *Supervising International Research Students*. London: Society for Research into Higher Education.

Oost, H. (2003) *Circling Around a Question*. Utrecht: IVLOS Institute of Education, Utrecht University.

Oost, H. (2004) *Een onderzoek begeleiden*. Baarn: HB Uitgevers.

Oost, H. (2006) *Methods of Legal Research*. Tilburg: Tilburg Law School.

Oost, H., Sonneveld, H. and van Gestel, R. (2013) *Rubrics Final Assignment 2008: Evaluation Criteria*. Tilburg: Tilburg Law School.

Pawson, R. and Tilley, N. (2008) *Realistic Evaluation*. London: Sage.

Perlberg, A. (1976) The use of laboratory systems in improving university teaching. *Higher Education*, 5: 135–51.

Phillips, E.M. and Johnson, C.G. (2022) *How to Get a PhD: A Handbook for Students and Their Supervisors* (7th edn). Maidenhead: Open University Press.

Punch, K.F. (2016) *Developing Effective Research Proposals* (3rd edn). London: Sage.

Roberts, A. (n. d.) Advice about writing a report, a dissertation or a thesis. Available at: http://studymore.org.uk/reports.htm (accessed 23 Sept. 2021).

Robinson, A. (2010) *Sudden Genius? The Gradual Path to Creative Breakthroughs*. Oxford: Oxford University Press.

Seldin, P. (1976) Teaching professors how to teach. Paper presented at the Second International Conference on Improving University Teaching, Heidelberg.

Snieder, R. and Larner, K. (2009) *The Art of Being a Scientist: A Guide for Graduate Students and Their Mentors*. Cambridge: Cambridge University Press.

Sonneveld, H. (1997) *Promotoren, promovendi en de academische selectie. De collectivisering van het Nederlandse promotiestelsel*. Amsterdam: Amsterdam University Press.
Sonneveld, H. (2009) *Brief aan een startende promovendus*. Utrecht: Medisch-Onderwijskundig Promovendi Netwerk / Nederlands Centrum voor de Promotieopleiding.
Sonneveld, H. (2014) *Supervisors at Work: Guidance of PhD Candidates at the Graduate School of Electrical Engineering, Mathematics and Computer Science*. Delft: Graduate School EEMCS.
Sonneveld, H. (2015) *Verslag project Langpromoveerders*. Tilburg: Tilburg Law School.
Sonneveld, H., Hello, E. and Schoot, R. van de. (2011) *Promovendimonitor 2011. Promovendi van de Universiteit Utrecht. Hun oordeel over opleiding, begeleiding en onderzoeksfaciliteiten*. Utrecht: Centrum voor Onderwijs en Leren / Expertisecentrum Graduate Schools Universiteit Utrecht.
Sonneveld, H. and Scager, K. (2008) *De Kwaliteit van de Promotiebegeleiding bij het Onderzoeksinstituut Geschiedenis en Cultuur – Evaluatierapport*. Utrecht: Ivlos/Nederlands Centrum voor de Promotieopleiding.
Stebbins, R.A. (2001) *Exploratory Research in the Social Sciences*. Thousand Oaks, CA: Sage Publications.
Turabian, K.L. (2007) *A Manual for Writers of Research Papers, Theses, and Dissertations* (7th edn). Chicago: The University of Chicago Press.
Verschuren, P. and Doorewaard, H. (2005) *Designing a Research Project*. Utrecht: Lemma.
Watts, M. (2001) The Holy Grail: In pursuit of the dissertation proposal, University of California. Available at: https://dusk.geo.orst.edu/prosem/PDFs/InPursuitofPhD.pdf. (accessed 22 Aug. 2021).
Wright Mills, C. (1970) *The Sociological Imagination*. Oxford: Oxford University Press.

Index

Page numbers in italics are figures; with 't' are tables; in bold are the appendices.

Abbott, B.B. 65, 125, 128
abstracts 101, **169–70**, **171**, **180**
action summaries 45–6
admission of doctoral candidates 13–15, 23–5
aftercare 92
anxieties 76
appendices
   A (literature tips) 30, **145–7**
   B (Proposal Lab prospectus) 26, **148–53**, **151t**
   C (example of a Proposal Lab Schedule) **154–9t**
   D (Snapshot) 5t, 24, 56, 87, 98, *98*, **160–2**
   E (Rough Topic Exploration Matrix) 55, 56, 86, 87, 90, **163**, **164t**
   F (planning the well-reasoned topic choice and proposal design) 5t, 6t, 46, 99, **165–6t**, **166–8t**
   G (criteria for evaluating research questions) 6t, 7t, 39, 40, 44, 45, 59, 62, 100, 104, 105, 123, **169–76**
   H (Well-reasoned Topic Choice) 6t, 56, **177–8**
   I (Proposal Halfway form) 6t, 7t, 39, 45, 82, 101, **179–83**
   J (Disciplinary Embedding Assignment) 106, 107, 109–10, 111, **184–5**
   K (Question Practicum) 6t, 7t, 61, 101, 121, **186–7t**, **188**
   L (evaluating individual research training) 5t, 47, 59, 60, 94, 100, 101, 113, 114, 116, 117–18, 119, **189–91**, **191–2t**, **193**, **194t**
   M (SWOT analysis for halfway) 9t, **195**
   N (expectations in view of a 4 year PhD project) 40–1, 104, **196–200t**
   O (Planning Matrix PhD trajectory) 40, 104, **202–3t**

   P (SWOT analysis in view of future PhD project) 79, **204–5t**
   Q (Training and Supervision Plan) **202t**, **206–10t**
application, and Proposal Lab 23, **149**
assignments, Proposal Lab **150**, **151–2**, **165–6t**, **166–7t**
Atkinson, P., *Supervising the Doctorate* 147
attrition 15–16
Aveyard, H. 57, 59, 106–7, 111, 119, 145

Becker, Howard 55, 76–7, 84, 146
bibliography **174**, **183**
Bizup, J, *The Craft of Research* 145–6
Booth, W.C. 55, 59, 63, 84, 110, 112, 123, 126
   The Craft of Research 66, 145–6
Bordens, K.S. 65, 125, 128
Bowen, W.G. 12
Brewer, R. 45, 100
   Your PhD Thesis 39
Bryman, A. 66–7, 68, 102, 115–16, 122–3
buffer time 43–4

calendar, Proposal Lab 27–30, **28–30t**
candidates, types 90–1, 135–6
Clinic model 2, 8–10, 9–10t, 10t, 17, **195**
collaboration 21
communication, problems with 74–5
community of practice *see* Proposal Lab
comparison 132
components of a proposal 39–40
concepts *see* hypotheses/propositions/concepts
consistency **174–5**
context 132
Corbin, J. 132
core questions 39, 61, 102, **180**
critical appraisal, of literature 114, 117–18, **191–3**

data 103, 129–33, **183**
Delamont, S., *Supervising the Doctorate* 147
design, research 66–9, **173**
disciplinary embedding 56–7, 109–13, **152–3**, **184–5**
diversity 50
  of subjects 88t
Doorewaard, H. 67

Eco, Umberto 39, 43
'80 percent ready model' 48
essential tension 21–2
evaluation
  on PhD student's work 139–41, 140t
  of Proposal Lab programme 139
  of proposals 68
  self- 76, 78, 85, 89t
  of supervision 53
expectations, from supervisors 48–9
external PhD candidates 8

feedback, Proposal Lab 23, 86–92, 88–9t, 119–21, 134
final proposal 39, 40, *42*, *98*, 104, 134, **161t**
finances 2, 71, 79
FitzGerald, W.T., *The Craft of Research* 145–6
flexibility 43, 50–1

Gestel, Rob van 40, 104
Glaser, B.G. 125
Gosling, P., *Mastering Your PhD* 146
Greenhalgh, T. 117, 145
group approach 33
Guetzkow, J. 60
  What is Originality 104, 105
guides, PhD 75–6

Hunt, J. 146–7
hypotheses/propositions/concepts 66–7, 103, 124–5, **182**

independence 51
interviewing 25, **153**
  Proposal Lab session 93–7, *98*, 99, **189–90**
  for supervisors 46–7
intervision 44–5, 46t
introduction (PhD thesis) 8, 122

Johnson, Colin, *How to Get a PhD* 47, 145
journey to a proposal *see* roadmap to a proposal

knowledge 22–3, **149**

Laboratory model 17
  see also Proposal Lab
Lamont, M., *What is Originality* 104
Larner, K., *The Art of Being a Scientist* 147
literature
  on PhD proposals 30, **145–7**
  review 56–60, 98, *98*, 99, 107–8, 111–12, 114–19, *115*, **193–4**, **194t**
  search 106–13, **153**, **190–1**
Loehle, Craig 112
Lovitts, Barbara 12–13
  Making the Implicit Explicit 40, 146

Machine Trick 76–7, 81
Mallard, G., *What is Originality* 104
Manathunga, C. 138
meetings 72–3
  Proposal Lab feedback 86–92, 88–9t, 119–21
Meltzoff, J. 124
methods 103, **173**, **183**
mini-courses 17
Mirande, M.J.A. 17–18

Nhlengethwa, S. 146
Noordam, B., *Mastering Your PhD* 146
note-taking 59, 114, 116–17, **157t**

Oost, Heinze 40, 104, 129
originality 60–1, 102, 104–5, **172**, **181**

Parry, O., *Supervising the Doctorate* 147
paths to proposal 33–6, 34–5t
Pawson, R. 64, 124, 125
peer review 21, 35
peer support 44, 46, 71–5, 88t
PhD journey 5–7t
Phillips, Estelle, *How to Get a Phd* 47, 145
planning a PhD 2, 22, 41–2, *42*, 46
  candidates'/supervisors' plans 3–4, 3–4t, 32, 33, 34–5t
  and the Proposal Lab 97–9, *98*, 103–4, **202–3**

preconditions 54–5
process 132
Proposal Halfway 38, 40, 81, *98*, 99, 103, 104, 134, **153**, **183**
  reflection **175**
  SWOT analysis 70–1
Proposal Lab 18–19, 30, 35–6
  admission 13–15, 23–5
  calendar 27–30, 28–30t
  didactic background 17–22
  goals 16–17
  history 12–13
  individual feedback meetings 86–92, 88–9t
    well-reasoned topic choice 119–21
    see also Proposal Halfway
  interviewing researchers/planning the proposal 93–100, *98*
  literature
    review 57–8, *98*, *98*, 99, 114–19, *115*, **152**
    search 106–13
  objectives 22–3
  proposal 100–6
  prospectus 25–6
  research design 128–34
  research questions 121–4
  roadmap of the journey 26–7, *26–7*
  and student attrition 15–16
  support for students 2, 3, 11
  and theory 65, 124–8, **172–3**
  and topics 80–6, *98*, 119–21
propositions *see* hypotheses
prospectus, Proposal Lab (Appendix B) 26, **148–53**, 151t

Question Practicum (Appendix K) 6t, 7t, 61, 101, 121, **186–7t**, **188**
questions
  core 39, 61, 102, **180**
  research 61–3, 68, 69, *98*, 101, 121–4, **153**, **171**, **175–6**, **180–1**
  see also Question Practicum

reflection **175**
relevance 104–5
reliability 66
research design 66–9, **173**
  Proposal Lab 128–34
research files 41, 46, 83–4

research questions 61–3, 68, 69, *98*, 101, 121–4, **153**, **171**, **175–6**, **180–1**
roadmap to a proposal 26–7, *26–7*, 31–2, 36–46, *37–8*, *42*, 45t
  end of the proposal journey 78–9
  preconditions 53–4
  problems and concerns 70–7
  stages 54–69
  supervisors/convenors 46–53
Robinson, Andrew, 'Sudden Genius?' 82
Rough Topic Exploration Matrix (App. E) 55–6, 86, 87, 90, **163**, **164t**
Rudenstine, N.L. 12

schedule 72, **154–9t**
self-evaluation 76, 78, 85, 89t
Session 1 (Proposal Lab) research topics 80–6
Session 2 (Proposal Lab) meeting and interviewing researchers/planning the proposal 93–100, 98
Session 3 (Proposal Lab) the PhD proposal 100–6
Session 4 (Proposal Lab) searching for the important literature 106–13
Session 5 (Proposal Lab) literature review 114–19, 115
Session 6 (Proposal Lab) research questions 121–4
Session 7 (Proposal Lab) theory/hypothesis/claim 124–8
Session 8 (Proposal Lab) research design 128–34
skills, and Proposal Lab 23, **149**
Snapshot 5t, 24, 56, 87, 98, *98*, **160–2**
Snieder, R., *The Art of Being a Scientist* 147
solo preparation 33
Stebbins, R.A. 83
Strauss, A. 132
Strauss, A.L. 125
strengths/weaknesses 79, 87, 88–9t, 91–2
summaries 55–6
supervisors 1, 46–53, 85
  advice from colleagues on 72, 73–4
  choosing 22, *98*
  and the Machine Trick 77
  and original study 105
  support for students 2–11, 3–4t, 5–7t, 9–10t, 10t

training and supervision plan **206–10t**
support, for students 2–11, 3–4t, 5–7t, 9–10t, 10t
SWOT analysis
  Proposal Halfway 70–1, **195**
  in view of a (future) PhD project **204–5t**

theory 63–6, 102, **172–3**
  and Proposal Lab 124–8, **182**
Tilley, N. 64, 124, 125
time 72, 73, 76
title of the research project 101
tools of the trade programme 17
topics 54–5
  and Proposal Lab 5t, 6t, 46, 80–6, *98*, 99, **165–6t**, **166–8t**, **177–8**

Rough Topic Exploration Matrix (App. E) 55–6, 86, 87, 90, **163**, **164t**
Training and Supervision Plan **206–10t**
transparency 131
types of students/PhD candidates 90–1, 135–6

underperformance 136–41, 140t

validity 67
Verschuren, P. 67

Watts, M. 45
weaknesses *see* strengths/weaknesses
Williams, J.M., *The Craft of Research* 145–6
Wright Mills, C. 41, 83

www.ingramcontent.com/pod-product-compliance
Lightning Source LLC
Chambersburg PA
CBHW051116230426
43667CB00014B/2599